Seventy Years of Issues

Historical Vocal 78rpm Pressings from Original Masters 1931-2001

Compiled with notes by
Tom Peel and John Stratton

Foreword by The Earl of Harewood

DUNDURN PRESS
TORONTO • OXFORD

Editorial Co-ordinator: Anthony Hawke
Design: V. John Lee
Photography: Giulio M. Buttino
Technical Assistance: Thomas Loree
Printer: Friesens Corporation

Canadian Cataloguing in Publication Data

Stratton, John, 1931-
Seventy years of issues: historical vocal 78rpm pressings from original masters 1931-2001

ISBN 1-55002-352-7

1. Vocal music – Discography. 2. Sound recordings – Catalogs.
I. Peel, Tom, 1939- . II. Title.

ML156.4.V7S9 12 2001 016.78206'8'0266 C00-932080-6

THE CANADA COUNCIL FOR THE ARTS SINCE 1957 | LE CONSEIL DES ARTS DU CANADA DEPUIS 1957

Canada

ONTARIO ARTS COUNCIL
CONSEIL DES ARTS DE L'ONTARIO

This book was made possible through the generous assistance of The Historic Singers Trust, and Dr. John Stratton.

We acknowledge the support of the Canada Council for the Arts and the Ontario Arts Council for our publishing program. We also acknowledge the financial support of the Government of Canada through the Book Publishing Industry Development Program, The Association for the Export of Canadian Books, and the Government of Ontario through the Ontario Book Publishers Tax Credit Program.

Care has been taken to trace the ownership of copyright material used in this book. The author and the publisher welcome any information enabling them to rectify any references or credit in subsequent editions.

J. Kirk Howard, President

Printed and bound in Canada.
Printed on recycled paper.

www.dundurn.com

Dundurn Press
8 Market Street
Suite 200
Toronto, Ontario, Canada
M5E 1M6

Dundurn Press
73 Lime Walk
Headington, Oxford,
England
OX3 7AD

Dundurn Press
2250 Military Road
Tonawanda NY
U.S.A. 14150

Dedicated to the memory of Emilio de Gogorza

ACKNOWLEDGEMENTS

This work would not have been possible without the full support and advice of the Historic Masters Committee: The Earl of Harewood, Stanley Henig, Richard Bebb, Eliot Levin, John Stratton, Michael Henstock, Tom Peel and Roger Beardsley.

It would also be a much less accurate work without the previous efforts of (especially) William Moran, Julian Morton Moses, Alan Kelly and the dozens of scholarly contributors to *The Record Collector* over the past fifty-odd years.

John Stratton in particular wishes to thank Thomas Loree and John Rutherford for their secretarial assistance in putting the layout together, and Giulio M. Buttino for the great patience exercised in photographing original labels.

CONTENTS

FOREWORD

The sin of envy is one from which collectors of old vocal records are by no means immune, and I was first affected by it when I was a schoolboy before the Second World War and read of the re-issues of recordings by legendary singers which were out of my reach because they were mainly published on the other side of the Atlantic. Eventually, I got hold of one or two by Lilli Lehmann (published in Europe) and very gradually, over the years, built up a collection of those other coveted (envied?) re-issues.

Many of them turned out to be marvelous, and others raised intriguing questions that were, in those distant days, not always easy to answer. Who, for instance, was Jacques Urlus, whose electrical recording re-issued by Parlophone made such an impact? It took years to answer that question satisfactorily, but the answer provoked a satisfying search for his earlier recordings.

Re-issues on both sides of the Atlantic, always in first-rate pressings, lead post-war to the first group of recordings sponsored by the British Institute of Recorded Sound, and those in turn were succeeded in England by a long list sponsored by an organisation set up especially for the purpose and simply called Historic Masters.

The aim now, as it was in the past, is to concentrate on recordings of real quality and established rarity, many of them unissued at the time of recording. As well as being rare, they sometimes turn out to shed light on facets of operatic history. I wholeheartedly support the aim, and the more often we satisfy the relevant criteria, the better that band of dedicated collectors will be satisfied.

This catalogue of all re-issues since those early days of the 1930s is invaluable and represents a genuine labour of love. In the end, such issues aim not only to give satisfaction, because they make available once again what is incredibly hard to find in its original format, and perhaps even never available before; each issue is not only, with any luck, beautiful in itself but also indicates why certain recorded artists were prominent in their time. Re-issues can never quite take the place of an original, with all its overtones of exclusivity, but they can continue to give real satisfaction to collectors just as much interested in hearing what the disc contains as in owning what other people don't possess. In this way, sometimes even the sin of envy can be, at least temporarily, transformed.

The Earl of Harewood

PREFACE

We have made every effort to provide complete and accurate information. Inevitably, there are some omissions and mistakes. Tom Peel has worked out a system of distinguishing re-pressings from dubbings. There have been quite a few cases where one side of a record has been a re-pressing and the other side has been a dubbing. Every effort has been made to distinguish these, and let us hope that the layout he has devised is both clear and usefully set forth.

Tom Peel has decided that where we have a dubbed reverse, details of that dubbing are given, but the issue number is placed in parentheses (see e.g. IRCC 54 rr).

Some Fonotipia dates have the entry 'FD' before the date. Dates thus shown are factory dates, not recording dates. Numbers in square brackets are unconfirmed. All dates are in the British, not American, fashion; i.e. day-month-year.

The layout is simple and cast in such a way that one's eye can run down any particular column — be it singers' names, matrix numbers or issue numbers — without confusion. Where sides have been re-issued by more than one company, there are cross-references in italics at the end of the appropriate entries. Issue numbers shown in brackets were allocated but not used. Titles are given in the language as sung; the original words follow in brackets; Russian titles are given in the accepted English/French translation; Flotow's 'Martha' presents its own difficulties, and titles are usually given in the standard Italian form. Verdi and Donizetti 'French' operas are translated from the Italian, where known.

As the appearance of these various issues has continued practically unabated over the decades, and at some times more than one organisation was producing such records, there has, by now, been quite an accumulation, and it is clear that collectors are rather unclear as to by whom and just what has been issued. During most of the period, these issues have been small pressing runs, sometimes very small, particularly in the first decade or so - perhaps not even 100. The records over the years have been virtually handmade, virtually every copy inspected for quality. Little wonder that these records now are much sought-after by collectors and often bring quite high prices on auction lists. Indeed, the entire category of records we are considering has been very well pressed, which precedent Historic Masters, assisted by EMI, is trying its best to continue. We owe it especially to Michael

Henstock, a distinguished metallurgist, as well as record-collector and member of the Historic Masters Committee, as currently attending at EMI's Hayes pressing factory during the period when the issue runs are being pressed and thereby exercising on-the-spot quality control. Sometimes several stampers for a single item have to be produced just to get the small number of discs of our production.

The earliest of the issues we are considering were the pressings of Lilli Lehman's operatic recordings that Desmond Shawe-Taylor was involved with producing and which the Parlophone Company pressed in England in 1931. The following year, William H. Seltsam of Bridgeport, Connecticut, founded the International Record Collectors Club (IRCC) and, over the next 20 years, was the main producer of these semi-private issues. From him they were obtained either by subscription or from fairly regular bulletins. In the earliest days, both Columbia and Victor in America pressed records for the IRCC, but by far the majority of his issues from original masters were done by the Victor Company and are therefore often referred to as IRCC Victors. They had lovely silver Victor labels with dark blue printing. Frequently a photograph of the singer of the recording was attached, and, in quite a number of cases, the labels were individually autographed.

From quite early on, Seltsam (who was never very happy about such things) had a rival in the person of William Speckin of Chicago. He too, over a period of several years, produced similar-size runs of pressings, though seldom overlapping the IRCC production, under the aegis of the Historic Record Society (HRS). These, in general, had gold labels with red lettering. The pressing quality was equal in both. Though the HRS produced quite a few records (many of them, incidentally, also autographed), the number was not as great in total as the IRCC issues. Both organisations brought out a few unpublished titles, but any large access to Victor unpublished material has not yet occurred. The Historic Masters, on the other hand, particularly in the last several years, has issued a great many unpublished titles derived from EMI's Hayes archive. The Historic Masters committee is constantly engaged in searching for such material.

In the late 1930s, contact was made with the firm of Carl Lindstrom in Berlin, which had become heir of surviving early Odeon and Fonotipia matrices, and, at this period, quite a few items were pressed for the two organisations in 10 3/4-inch format. Those done for the IRCC generally did not specify the IRCC, though many of those done for HRS did. At about the same time, Parlophone and Odeon built up a series of historical re-issues which were available in their catalogues until the Second World War years, including a good many historically important recordings, quite a number of them 10 ¾-inch.

By the end of the Second World War and the period of the advent of the 45 rpm disc and the LP, the Victor Company seems no longer to have been interested in small runs of records for Seltsam and Speckin. Indeed, Victor began a historical re-issue series of its own: the Heritage Series, very glossily put out, with the records pressed in red plastic and marketed in large glamorous gold envelopes. Not to be thwarted, however, Seltsam and Speckin communicated with EMI, who, over the next several years, until the early 1950s, produced many more pressings for them. Later, this became known as the Archive Series, with white labels and gold lettering (often referred to as the VA and VB series). Quite unexpectedly, about 1951, EMI gathered all the material together and produced a nicely got-up bulletin that was distributed with *Gramophone* magazine and elsewhere. In a short time, these records, containing a great many fine and important items, became widely distributed. For many of us, this provided virtually the backbone of our historical collections. The Archive Series was added to for a short time longer, and later items are more elusive, though not exactly rare. About the same time — the early 1950s — a man in Philadelphia whose name was Addison Foster approached EMI for a series of pressings to be made especially for him and his American Gramophone Society (AGS). This event marked virtually the termination of the IRCC's and the HRS's involvement with producing historical pressings. Addison Foster's AGS records had mauve labels with gold lettering. Both Victor and Gramophone Company matrices were utilised, and Victor material, if not already there, was sent over to England for the pressings to be made. Interestingly, in a few cases, there were reissues of things put out earlier by IRCC pressed by Victor, and it was the IRCC versions of these matrices that found their way back to England. A fair number of hitherto unpublished things came out in the AGS series, though much was classics. The production of these reords continued throughout the mid-1950s. Addison Foster appears to have had some arrangement with EMI such that only he could obtain pressing runs. A few other things were, as it happened, sponsored, and these came out with navy-blue labels and gold lettering and were numbered ABHA for 10-inch and ABHB for 12-inch. Only eight such records came out: one 10-inch and seven 12-inch. They were obtainable from Addison Foster, and presumably from elsewhere. I certainly obtained all mine from him. At some point in the late 1950s, this rich vein dried up. The evidence is that Addison Foster had a number of further issues in view at this time and evidently there were a few test copies, now extremely elusive. One was AGSB 64, an Ancona disk coupling the 'Ernani' solo (CA4284, 88062) with the never generally available Death of Valentine from 'Faust' (C4992, unpublished except for IRCC). Another was AGSB 103, which consisted of two unpublished Pinza recordings ('Trovatore', 2A59746, and the Verdi Requiem, 2A51979). If there were others such as these, of which copies actually exist, I am not aware of them.

After this there was a long hiatus, until in the early 1970s, Richard Bebb masterminded a scheme by which the British Institute of Recorded Sound issued the first series of twenty Historic Masters. An advisory committee was set up under the Chairmanship of Lord Harewood whose diplomatic skills were much in evidence during protracted negotiations with EMI about the new project. The presence of Desmond Shawe-Taylor on the committee was a link to the very first re-issues some forty years previously. The first Historic Masters were pressed to the exact numbers subscribed and paid for in advance.

Although the BIRS made a substantial profit from the project in the 1970s, there were no arrangements in place for its continuation, and there was a long gap before the Historic Masters scheme was revived. At the time, the BIRS was an autonomous organization with a rotating governing body. Professor Stanley Henig became a member in the late 1970s and he brought together members of the former advisory committee. In due course this became the Board of Historic Masters Ltd, and was established as an independent company operating under licence from EMI. Once again Lord Harewood was Chairman and the key player in the necessary negotiations with both EMI and the BIRS. Professor Henig became the Secretary. Since the mid 1980s, Historic Masters have continued to appear at regular intervals, reaching number 156 in the millennium year. Of these, HM 1 to HM 20, and issues from HM 100 onwards, have been pressed at the EMI factory. HM 21 to HM 99 were produced by Eliot Levin of Symposium Records. He has made a significant contribution to resolving the many problems involved in pressing from original metal parts of 78rpm records. The 156 discs included a certain number of 10 ¾-inch items, though they have had to be pressed in 12-inch format, and also, from time to time, some 10-inch material, though sometimes it too in 12-inch format. Although we of Historic Masters have had access only to EMI material in the Hayes archive for our issues, we know that Victor still possesses a large number of historical matrices, including many of European (i.e. EMI) origin. Quite a few, especially unpublished things, were pressed privately about 15 years ago. We are fortunate that both these large caches of historical recordings seem to be still in pretty good shape as metals. There are one or two interesting anomalies in all this. Of great interest are the four discs of recordings by Blanche Marchesi that she made for her own distribution when over 70 in 1936 and 1937. Though recorded in London by EMI (HMV), these have not survived at Hayes. However, three of the four disks were issued at the same time by the IRCC, the labels autographed by Marchesi. The metal parts for these have survived at Victor and yield perfect vinyl pressings.

We may hope that the Historic Masters' semi-private enterprise of reissuing original vocal recordings may continue and that we may yet find rare and unpublished material at Hayes, and perhaps one day gain access to the Victor archives as well.

Tom Peel & John Stratton

Historical Vocal 78rpm Pressings from Original Masters

Listing by Issuer

DESMOND SHAWE-TAYLOR (Co-Sponsor with 'The Gramophone')
All Lilli LEHMANN (Odeon)

A) Ux 52577 *Don Giovanni : Don Ottavio, son morta* (Mozart)
(xB 1478) 20- 7-06

A) Ux 52578 *Don Giovanni : Or sai che l'onore* (Mozart)
(xB 1479) 20- 7-06

B) Ux 52741 *La Traviata : Ah fors' è lui* (Verdi)
(xB 2976) 18- 6-07

B) Ux 52742 *La Traviata : Sempre libera* (Verdi)
(xB 2977) 18- 6-07

C) Ux 52698 *Norma : Casta diva* (Bellini)
(xB 2978) 18- 6-07

C) Ux 52606 *Norma : Ah ! sì fa core* (Bellini) w.Hedwig HELBIG (s)
(xB 3063) 25- 6-07

D) AA 57895 *Die Entführung aus dem Serail : Marten aller arten* (Mozart)
(xxB 3048) 22- 6-07

D) AA 57896 *Die Entführung aus dem Serail : Ach ich liebte* (Mozart)
(xxB 2980) 18- 6-07

E) Ux 52576 *Don Giovanni : Fors' è un giorno il cielo* (Mozart)
(xB 3046) 22- 6-07 *HMA 105*

E) Ux 52575 *Don Giovanni : Non mi dir* (Mozart)
(xB 3045) 22- 6-07

F) Ux 52699 *La Traviata : Alfredo, Alfredo, in questo core* (Verdi)
(xB 3047) 22- 6-07 *HMB 144*

F) Ux 52600 *Così fan tutte : Ich erwähle mir den Muntern (Prenderò quel*
w.Hedwig HELBIG (s) *Brunettino)*(Mozart)
(xB 3061) 25- 6-07 *HMB 144*

G) Ux 52597 *Fidelio : Abscheulicher* (Beethoven)
(xB 3049) 22- 6-07 *HMB 59*

G) Ux 52598 *Crucifix* (Fauré) w.Hedwig HELBIG (s)
(xB 3065) 25- 6-07

H) AA 79300 *Fidelio : Komm' Hoffnung* (Beethoven)
(xxB 3050) 22- 6-07 *HMB 60*

H) AA 79301 *Fidelio : Ich folg'dem innern Triebe* (Beethoven)
w.Hedwig HELBIG (s)
(xxB 3051) 22- 6-07 *HMB 60*

J) Ux 52605 *Le Nozze di Figaro : Wenn die sanften Abendlüfte* (Mozart)
(xB 3060) 25- 6-07

J) Ux 50393 *Die Walküre : Du bist der lenz* (Wagner)
(xB 3147) 5- 7-07 *IRCC P PO 63*

NOTE : Odeon's initial issue numbers are shown on the left with the (letter) suffixes placed (in this issue) as pre-fixes.

The two items below were issued by Shawe-Taylor in association with 'Collectors Corner'

PO 2 Victor MAUREL (b)

Ninon (Tosti)

(XPh 69-2)* (FD) 23-11-04 F. 39247 *IRCC 9*

* The date shown is for Xph 69 and does not necessarily apply to Xph 69-2

Note: Some copies of this disc have Garbin's ZAZA aria replacing 'NINON'

Falstaff : Quand'ero paggio (Verdi)

(XPh 2332) 8- 1-07 F. 62016 *IRCC 4*

PO 18 Victor MAUREL (b)

Otello : Era la notte (Verdi)

(XPh 58-3) (FD) 21-11-04 F. 39042-2 *IRCC 4*

Don Giovanni : Deh, vieni alla finestra (Mozart)

(XPh 66) (FD) 21-11-04 F. 39041 *IRCC 9*

INTERNATIONAL RECORD COLLECTORS CLUB (IRCC)

UN-NUMBERED SERIES

IRCC A Ada ADINI (s)

Hérodiade : Il est doux, il est bon (Massenet)

(XPh 580-2) 1-12-12 F. 39216

Aïno ACKTÉ (s)

Si j'avais vos ailes (Messager)

(XPr 1-2) not known F. 39059 *PO 93*

IRCC B Giuseppe ANSELMI (t)

La Gioconda : Cielo e mar ! (Ponchielli)

(XXPh 2821) 4-11-07 F. 74029

La Bohème : Che gelida manina (Puccini)

(XXPh 2822) 4-11-07 F. 74032

IRCC C Alessandro BONCI (t)

I Puritani : A te o cara (Bellini)

[XXPh 394]* 19-10-05 F. 39084

* NOTE: 394-2 in wax therefore this date cannot be guaranteed

L'Elisir d'Amore : Una furtiva lagrima (Donizetti)

(XPh 153) F. 39083

IRCC D Maria BARRIENTOS (s)

Fra Diavolo : Or son sola (Quel bonheur) (Auber)

(XPh 1632) 20- 2-06 F. 39538

Fra Diavolo : Già per la danza (Auber)

(XPh 1633) 20- 2-06 F. 39539

IRCC E Edmond CLÉMENT (t)

La Dame Blanche : Grand Air (Boieldieu)
[XPh 758] not known Od.56002
Victor MAUREL (b)
A year ago (d'Hardelot)
(XPh 2333) 8- 1-07 F. 62018

IRCC F Fernando DE LUCIA (t)
Mignon : Addio Mignon (Adieu Mignon, courage) (Thomas)
(549 c) c. - 9/10-05 G. 052111 *V. 15- 1024*
Maria GALVANY (s) Aristodemo GIORGINI (t)
L'Elisir d'Amore : Chiedi all'aura (Donizetti)
(551L) 1906 G. 054110
IRCC G Maria DE MACCHI (s)
Lucrezia Borgia : Com' è bello (Donizetti)
(XPh 1916) 28- 5-06 F. 39832
Poliuto : Aria de Paolina : Di qual soavi lagrime (Donizetti)
(XPh 2554) 17- 4-07 F. 39901
IRCC H Emmy DESTINN (s)
The Bartered Bride : Gern ja will ich dir vertrauen
(Kdybych se co takového) (Smetana)
(XPh 1018) 1905 F. 39424
Le Nozze di Figaro : Heilige Quelle (Porgi amor) (Mozart)
(BX 1662) 1906 Od. 50153
IRCC J Emmy DESTINN (s)
Robert le Diable : Geh sprach sie zu mir (Va ! dit elle) (Meyerbeer)
(xB 3612) 1907 Od. 64855
Robert le Diable : Eh'ich die Normandie verlassen
(Quand je quittai la Normandie) (Meyerbeer)
(xB 3613) 1907 Od. 64837
IRCC K Maria GALVANY (s)
Roméo et Juliette : Valse (It) *(Je veux vivre dans ce rêve)* (Gounod)
(1308 c) 1907 G. 053163
Lucia di Lammermoor : Splendon le sacri faci (Donizetti)
(1453½ c) -10-08 G. 053181
IRCC L Selma KURZ (s) Leopold DEMUTH (b)
Die Zauberflöte : Bei Männern (Mozart)
(13979 u) 1908 G. 2-44495
Mignon : Styrienne (Je connais un pauvre enfent) (Thomas)
(3991 h) 21-12-05 G. 43737
IRCC M Lilli LEHMANN (s)
Du bist die Ruh' (Schubert)
(xB 3137) 2- 7-07 Od. 50432
Egmont : Freudvoll und Leidvoll No :7 *(Klärchens Lied)* (Schubert)

(xB 3142) 2- 7-07 Od. 50390

IRCC N Lilli LEHMANN (s)

Du bist die Ruh' (Schubert)

(xB 3137) 2- 7-07 Od. 50432

Intermezzo (Schumann)

(xB 3133) 2- 7-07 Od. 50372

IRCC P Lilli LEHMANN (s)

Joshua : O hätt' ich Jubals Harf' (Handel)

(xB 3143) 2- 7-07 Od. 50392

Die Walküre : Du bist der Lenz (Wagner)

(xB 3147) 5- 7-07 Od. 50393

DST J PO 63

IRCC Q Lilli LEHMANN (s)

Auf dem Wasser zu singen (Schubert)

(xB 1304) 29- 6-06 Od. 50094 *HMA 59*

Egmont : Freudvoll und Leidvoll No :4 *(Klärchens Lied)* (Beethoven)

(xB 1306) 29- 6-06 Od. 50078

IRCC R . Lilli LEHMANN (s)

ss *Robert le Diable : Gnadenarie : (Robert, mein Geliebter)*

(Robert, toi que j'aime) (Meyerbeer)

(xxB 3148) 5- 7-07 Od. 80009

IRCC S Felia LITVINNE (s)

Aïda : Grâce pitié (I sacri nomi) (Verdi)

(XPh 691) not known F. 39217 *HMA 10*

Cavalleria Rusticana : Voi lo sapete o mamma (Mascagni)

(XPh 675) not known F. 39052 *HMA 10*

IRCC T Felia LITVINNE (s)

Lohengrin : Rêve de Elsa (Einsam in trüben Tagen) (Wagner)

(XPh 676) not known F. 39182 *HMA 93*

L'Africaine : Air du sommeil (Sur mes genoux) (Meyerbeer)

(XPh 695) not known F. 39218

IRCC U Victor MAUREL (b)

Le rondel de l'adieu (de Lara)

(XPh 67) (FD) 21-11-04 F. 39246

Mandolinata (Paladilhe)

(XPh 68-2) (FD) 21-11-04 F. 39245

IRCC V Rosina STORCHIO (s)

Don Pasquale : Quel guardo il cavaliere (Donizetti)

(XPh 1500) 2-12-05 F. 39400 *PO 121*

Don Pasquale : So anch'io la virtù magica (Donizetti)

(XPh 1501) 2-12-05 F. 39401 *PO 121*

IRCC W Salomea KRUSCENISKI

Loreley : Da che tutta (Catalani)
(Xph 4813) F. 92939
Madama Butterfly : Un bel dì vedremo (Puccini)
(Xph 4816) F. 92940

INTERNATIONAL RECORD COLLECTORS CLUB (IRCC)

IRCC 1 Geraldine FARRAR (s)
The Chestnut tree (Der Nussbaum) (Schumann)
(B 27730-2) 3- 4-23 V. Unp. 1st. Issue
Poème d'amour No.3 : *Ouvre tes yeux bleus* (Massenet)
(B 26870-2) 8- 9-22 V. Unp. 1st. Issue
IRCC 2 Dame Nellie MELBA
Rigoletto : Caro nome (Verdi)
(Melba 22) - 3-04 G. 03025
Otello : Piangea cantando ... Salce (Verdi)
(CR 417) 8-6-26 G. 2-053263
IRCC 4 Victor MAUREL (b)
Otello : Era la notte (Verdi)
(XPh 58-3) * (FD) 21-11-04 F. 39042 *PO 18*
* There were two editions of this side - the 1st master being supplied by Columbia and the 2nd by Lindstrom's Odeon.
Falstaff : Quand'ero paggio (Verdi)
(XPh 2332) 8- 1-07 F. 62016 *PO 2*
IRCC 5 Emma CALVÉ (s)
Carmen : Séguidille (Bizet)
(2062 R (b)) - 7-02 G.3285
Jeanne GERVILLE-RÉACHE (ms)
Carmen : En vain pour éviter les réponses a mères (Bizet)
(B 8335-1) 30-10-09 V. 87039
IRCC 6 Ernest VAN DYCK (t)
Ich grolle nicht (Schumann)
(XPh 535) 1905 F. 39100
Du bist wie eine Blume (Schumann op.25 No.24)
(XPh 539) 1905 F. 39101
IRCC 7 Dame Nellie MELBA (s) John McCORMACK (t)
Mario SAMMARCO (b)
Faust : Terzetto finale : Alerte ! ... Anges purs (Gounod)
(4190 f) - 5-10 G. Unp. 1st. Issue
F. 15-1019
Dame Nellie MELBA (s)
Le Temps des Lilas (Chausson)

(Z 7325 f) 6- 5-13 G. 2-033037

IRCC 8 Marcella SEMBRICH (s)
La Sonnambula : Ah ! non giunge (Bellini)
(B 1902-2) 19-11-04 V. 81047

Lilian BLAUVELT (s)
Les Vêpres Siciliennes : Bolero (Merci, Compagnons) (Verdi)
(B 424-2) 13- 4-05 V. 81067 *AGSA 4*

IRCC 9 Victor MAUREL (b)
Don Giovanni : Serenata (Deh, vieni alla finestra) (Mozart)
(XPh 66) (FD) 21-11-04 F. 39041 *PO 18*
Ninon (Tosti)
(XPh 69-2)* (FD) 23-11-04 F. 39247 *PO 2*
* Date for Xph 69 and does not necessarily apply to Xph 69-2

IRCC 10 Adelina PATTI (s)
Le Nozze di Figaro : Voi che sapete (Mozart)
(537 f) -12-05 G. 03051
Don Giovanni : Batti, batti o bel Masetto (Mozart)
(541 f) -12-05 G. 03055

IRCC 11 Elena GERHARDT (ms)
Heimweh (Wolf)
(5167 h) 1907 G. 2-43182
Und willst du deinen Liebsten sterben seh'n (Wolf)
(5169 h) 1907 G. 2-43183

IRCC 12 Olive FREMSTAD (s)
Tannhäuser : Dich, teure Halle (Wagner)
(30635-2) 21- 1-11 Col. 30635 *AF 2*
Lohengrin : Elsas Traum (Einsam in trüben Tagen) (Wagner)
(30645-1) 30- 1-11 Col. 30645 *AF 3*

IRCC 13 Mario ANCONA (b)
I Pagliacci : Prologo (Sì può ?) (Leoncavallo)
(C 4271-1) 27- 2-07 V. 88055
Sérénade de Don Juan (Tchaikovsky)
(C 6057-1) 26- 3-08 V. 88168

IRCC 14 Geraldine FARRAR (s)
Königskinder : Weisst noch das grosse Nest ? (Humperdinck)
(C 12737-1) 19-12-12 V. 88412
Königskinder : Lieber Spielmann (Humperdinck)
(C 12736-1) 19-12-12 V. 88405

IRCC 15 Celestina BONINSEGNA (s) Fernando DE LUCIA (t)
Faust : Tardi si fa (Il se fait tard) (Gounod)
(213m) c. 6-10-04 G. 054043

Celestina BONINSEGNA (s) Giovanni VALLS (t)
Aïda : Fuggiam gli ardori inospiti (Verdi)

(215m) 1904 G. 054044

IRCC 16 Emmy DESTINN (s)
Salome : Jochanaan, ich bin verliebt in deinen Lieb (R.Strauss)
(4870 h) 1907 G.43874
Salome : Dein Haar ist Grässlich (R.Strauss)
(4871 h) 1907 G.43875

IRCC 17 Dame Nellie MELBA (s)
Elaine : L'amour est pur (Bemberg)
(690 c) 7- 7-06 G. Unp. 1st. Issue
Adelina PATTI (s)
La Calasera (Yradier)
(684 ½ c) - 6-06 G. 03085 1st. Issue
VB 40

IRCC 18 Antonio SCOTTI (b)
Falstaff : L'onore (Verdi)
(C 8286-1) 7-10-09 V. 88195
Rigoletto : Deh, non parlare al misero (Verdi)
Don Giovanni : Finch'han dal vino (Mozart)
(C 1094-1) 10- 3-04 V. 85031 *AGSB 24*

IRCC 19 Blanche ARRAL (s)
I Lombardi (Jérusalem) : Polonaise (Quelle ivresse)) (Verdi)
- 5-09 V. 74146 *V. 15- 1016*
Faust : Air des bijoux (Gounod)
- 5-09 V. 74147 *V. 15-1016*

IRCC 20 Emma EAMES (s) Emilio DE GOGORZA (b)
Don Giovanni : Là ci darem la mano (Mozart)
(C 3170-2) 9- 3-06 V. 89005
Le Nozze di Figaro : Crudel, perchè finora (Mozart)
(C 6967) 6- 4-09 V. 89023

IRCC 21 Anton VAN ROOY (b)
Tannhäuser : Wolfram's Ansprache (Blick' ich umher) (Wagner)
(2496 f) 1908 G. 042165
Tannhäuser : Als du im kühnem Sange (Wagner)
(2497 f) 1908 G. 042166

IRCC 22 Zelie DE LUSSAN (s)
Mignon : Connais-tu le pays ? (Thomas)
(A2188 - B 19-1)* 17- 5-03 V. 2188 V. 64005
Carmen : Habañera (Bizet)
(A2198 - B 18-1)* 17- 5-03 V. 2198 V. 64004
* 'A' matrices re-numbered as 'B' - both versions shown.

IRCC 23 Emma JUCH (s)
Lohengrin : Elsas Traum (Einsam in trüben Tagen) (Wagner)

(C 1293-1) 7- 5-04 V. 85033
La Serenata (Tosti)
(C 1294-1) 7- 5-04 V. 85034

IRCC 24 Fernando DE LUCIA (t)
La Traviata : De' miei bollenti spiriti (Verdi)
(622c) c. 1- 5-06 G. 052129 *V. 15- 1024*
Charles DALMORÈS (t)
Carmen : La fleur que tu m'avais jetée (Bizet)
(C 4249-3) 24-10-12 V. 85122 *V. 15-1013*

IRCC 25 Pol PLANÇON (bs)
Philèmon et Baucis : Au bruit des lourds marteaux (Gounod)
(B 2200-1) 24- 1-05 V. 81056
Le Chalet : Vallons de l'Helvatia (Adam)
(B 1050-1) 27- 2-04 V. 81037 *AGSA 32*

IRCC 26 Johanna GADSKI (s)
Der Fliegende Holländer : Senta's Ballad (Traft ihr das Schiff) (Wagner)
(C 5013-2) 6- 2-08 V. 88116
Aus meinen grossen Schmerzen (Franz op.5 No.1)
Liebchen ist da ! (Franz op.5 No.2)
(C 1258) 24- 1-01 V. 85032

IRCC 27 Luisa TETRAZZINI (s)
Aïda : Ritorna vincitor (Verdi)
(ac 5170 f) 11- 7-11 G. 2-053064
Lakmé : Bell song (It) *(Où va la jeune Hindoue ?)* (Delibes)
(ac 5166 f) 11- 7-11 G. 2-053056

IRCC 29 Geraldine FARRAR (s)
Roméo et Juliette : Walz : Je veux vivre dans ce rêve (Gounod)
(1315 r) 23- 6-06 G. 33618
Faust : Ah, que de bijoux (Gounod)
(3802 h) 27- 9-05 G. 43721

IRCC 30 Geraldine FARRAR (s)
Mefistofele : L'altra notte (Boïto)
(3800 h) 27- 9-05 G. 53425
Exsultate Jubilate : Alleluja (Mozart)
(B 12739-1) 19-12-12 V. 87126

IRCC 31 Ernestine SCHUMANN-HEINK (c)
La Clemenza di Tito : Parto, parto (Mozart)
(C 8231-3) 18- 9-09 V. 88196 *AGSB 21*
Rienzi : Gerechter Gott ! (Wagner)
(C 6478-1) 29- 9-08 V. 88140

IRCC 32 Emma EAMES (s)
Tosca : Vissi d'arte (Puccini)
(C 2401-1) 16- 3-05 V. 85059

Carmen : Je dis que rien ne m'épouvante (Bizet)
(C 3386-1) 14- 5-06 V. 88036 *AGSB 60*

IRCC 33 Adelina PATTI (s)
Pur dicesti (Lotti)
(538 f) -12-05 G. 03052
Ave Maria (Bach-Gounod)
(547 f) -12-05 G. Unp. 1st. Issue

IRCC 34 Dame Nellie MELBA (s)
Le Nozze di Figaro : Porgi amor (Mozart)
(Melba 26) - 5-04 G. 03028 *VB 40*
Chant Hindou (Bemberg)
(405 c) 20-10-04 G. 03036

IRCC 35 Dame Nellie MELBA (s)
Pastorale (Bizet)
(691 c) 7- 7-06 G. 03070
Fêtes Galantes No.1 *: En sourdine* (Debussy)
(C 6697-1) 1- 1-09 V. Unp. (G.03376)
1st. Issue

IRCC 36 Enrico CARUSO (t) Pasquale AMATO (b)
Luisa TETRAZZINI (s) Josephine JACOBY (c)
Rigoletto : Bella figlia dell'amore (Verdi)
(C 11447-4) 13- 2-12 V. Unp. G.2-054038
V. 15-1019
Emmy DESTINN (s) Louise Kirkby LUNN (c)
Aïda : Ebben qual nuovo fremito (Verdi)
(5145 f) 6- 7-11 G. 2-054023

IRCC 37 Lilli LEHMANN (s)
Les Huguenots : O glücklich land (Ô beau pays de la Touraine)
(Meyerbeer)
(xB 3149) 5- 7-07 Od. 50394
Mondnacht (Schumann)
(xB 3135) 2- 7-07 Od. 50373

IRCC 38 Maurice RENAUD (b)
Le Roi de Lahore : Promesse de mon avenir (Massenet)
(5779 p) 1906 G. 032045
Hérodiade : Vision fugitive (Massenet)
(5802 p) 1906 G. 032047

IRCC 39 Claudia MUZIO (s)
La Bohème : Mi chiamano Mimì (Puccini)
(298 aj) 20- 6-11 G. 053264 *AGSB 14*
Elda CAVALIERI (s)
La Gioconda : Suicidio (Ponchielli)
(C 3630-1) 27- 7-06 V. 74048

IRCC 40 Geraldine FARRAR (s)
Pur dicesti (Lotti)
(CVE 37348-1) 11- 1-27 V. Unp. 1st. Issue
Le Nozze di Figaro : E Susanna no vien ... Dove sono (Mozart)
(CVE 37349-1) 11- 1-27 V. Unp.*
* This side is (musically) incomplete - time ran out and the aria ends prematurely

IRCC 41 Geraldine FARRAR (s)
Auf Flügeln des Gesanges (Mendelssohn)
(BVE 37350-1) 11- 1-27 V. Unp. 1st. Issue
Christina's Lament (Dvorak)
(BVE 37356-1) 13- 1-27 V. Unp. 1st. Issue

IRCC 42 Johanna GADSKI (s)
Don Giovanni : In qual eccessi (Mozart)
(C 9489-1) 29- 9-10 V. 88253
Die Zauberflöte : Du also bist (Mozart) (w. Sparkes - Case - Mattfield)
(C 13131-3) 16- 4-13 V. 88441

IRCC 43 Emma EAMES (s)
Dopo (Tosti)
(C 11307-1) 27- 7-11 V. 88344 *AGSB 5*
Roméo et Juliette : Walz : Je veux vivre dans ce rêve (Gounod)
(C 4032-1) 13-11-06 V. 88011

IRCC 44 Emma EAMES (s) Louise HOMER (ms)
Lakmé: Dôme épais de jasmin (Delibes)
(C 6625-2) 25- 5-08 V. 89020
Lohengrin : Du, Armste (Wagner)
(C 6226-1) 25- 5-08 V. 89021

IRCC 45 Geraldine FARRAR (s)
La Traviata : Follie ! Follie ! ... Sempre libera (Verdi)
(1316 r) 23- 6-06 G. 53469
Cherry ripe (Horn)
(3798 h) 27- 9-05 G. 3620

IRCC 46 Blanche ARRAL (s)
El Bolero Grande (Vasseur)
not known 1909 V. 64107
Pauline DONALDA (s)
Faust : Air des bijoux (Gounod)
(8453 b) 9- 7-06 G. 33620 *AGSA 4*

IRCC 47 Dame Nellie MELBA (s)
Hamlet : Mad scene (1) (Thomas)
(Melba 20) - 3-04 G. 03023
Hamlet : Mad scene (2) (Thomas)
(Melba 21) - 3-04 G. 03024

IRCC 48 Marcella SEMBRICH (s) Emilio DE GOGORZA (b)
Hamlet : Doute de la Lumière (Thomas)
(C 4871-1) 9-10-07 V. 89010 *VB 29*
Marcella SEMBRICH (s)
Linda di Chamounix: O luce di quest'anima (Donizetti)
(C 6574-1) 2-11-08 V. 88142
V. 15- 1027 IRCC 49
Pol PLANÇON (bs)
La Sonnambula : Il mulino, la fonte ... Vi ravviso (Bellini)
(C 870-1) 23-12-03 V. 85018 *VB 12*
Don Carlos : Oui je suis ... Elle ne m'aime pas (Verdi)
(C 4343-1) 27- 3-07 V. 85116

IRCC 50 Olimpia BORONAT (s)
I Puritani : Qui la voce (Bellini)
(1775 L) 11-04 G. 53351 *VA 11*
Mireille : O d'amor messagera (Ô légère hirondelle) (Gounod)
(1773 L) 11-04 G. 53349

IRCC 51 Emmy DESTINN (s) Karl JÖRN (t)
Carmen : Tanzen will ich zu eurer Ehr (Je vais danser en vôtre honneur) (Bizet)
(0826 v) 14-10-08 G. 044099 (Set 18)
Carmen : Wie, du liebst mich nicht mehr (Tu ne m'aimes donc plus)(Bizet)
(0827 v) 14-10-08 G. 044104 (Set 36)

IRCC 52 Dame Nellie MELBA (s)
Down in the forest (Ronald)
(C 6698-1) 1- 1-09 V. Unp. (G. 03130)
1st. Issue *AGSB 67*
White sea mist (Ronald)
(C 6699-2) 1- 1-09 V. Unp. (G. 03134)
1st. Issue *AGSB 53*

IRCC 53 Sigrid ARNOLDSON (s)
Der Freischütz : Leise, leise (Weber)
(3580 r) 11-11-07 G.43972
La Traviata : Addio del passato (Verdi)
(12489 u) - 3-08 G. 53631

(IRCC 54 rr) Emma ALBANI (s)
Theodora : Angels ever bright and fair (Handel)
(321 L) 29-12-03 G. 03014

IRCC 54 Dame Nellie MELBA (s)
Les Anges pleurent (Bemberg)
(6151 b) 20-10-04 G. 3576

IRCC 55 Geraldine FARRAR (s)
Chant Vénetien (Bemberg)

(B 26734-2) 8- 9-22 V. Unp. (V. 87437)
1st. Issue

Serenade (Ständchen) (E) (R. Strauss)
(BVE 27731-3) 11- 1-27 V. Unp. 1st. Issue

IRCC 56 Olimpia BORONAT (s)
Don Pasquale : So anch'io la virtù magica (Donizetti)
(1506½ c) 1908 G. 053185
Les Huguenots : La tenera parola (A ce mot seul) (Meyerbeer)
(1517 c) 1908 G. 053187

IRCC 57 Fernando DE LUCIA (t)
Manon : Sogno (La rêve : En ferment les yeux) (Massenet)
(10515 b) 7- 9-07 G. 2-52607
AGSA 25
Carmela mia (de Curtis)
(13337 b) 21- 5-09 G. 2-52773

IRCC 58 Geraldine FARRAR (s)
Carmen : Je dis que rien ne m'épouvante (Bizet)
(C 6652-1) 8-12-08 V. 88144
Geraldine FARRAR (s) Giovanni MARTINELLI (t)
Carmen : Au quartier pour l'appel (Bizet)
(C 16021-4) 19- 5-15 (V. 88532) 1st. Issue
AGSB 51

IRCC 59 David BISPHAM (b)
Erlkönig (Schubert)
(30019-1) 1906 Col. 30019
Vittorio ARIMONDI (bs)
Faust : Serenata (Vous qui faites l'endormie) (Gounod)
(30099-1) 13- 4-07 Col.30099

IRCC 60 John McCORMACK (t)
Atalanta : Come, my beloved (Care selve) (Handel)
(Bb 5034-1) 4- 9-24 G. DA.645
Ridente la calma (Mozart)
(Bb 5096-2) 19- 9-24 G. 7-52278

IRCC 61 Geraldine FARRAR (s) Enrico CARUSO (t)
La Bohème : O soave fanciulla (Puccini)
(C 12751-1) 30-12-12 V. Unp. 1st. Issue
AGSB 50
Enrico CARUSO (t)
Les Pêcheurs de Perles : Mi par d'udire ancora (Je crois entendre encore)
(Bizet)
(268 i) - 4-04 G. 052066 *VB 44*

IRCC 62 John McCORMACK (t)
Feldeinsamkeit (Brahms op.86 No.2)

(Bb 5095-1) 10- 9-24 G. DA.635 *AGSA 50*

Komm' bald (Brahms op.75 No.5)

(Bb 5094-2) 10- 9-24 G. DA.628 *AGSA 50*

IRCC 63 Celestina BONINSEGNA (s)

Manon Lescaut : In quelle trine morbide (Puccini)

(2144 L) -10/11-04 G. 53372 *VA 4*

Ernani : Ernani, Ernani involami (Verdi)

(7321 b) 1905 G. 53417

IRCC 64 Fernando DE LUCIA (t) Josefina HUGUET (s)

Les Pêcheurs de Perles : Non hai compreso (Ton coeur n'a pas compris) (Bizet)

(621 c) c. - 5-06 G. 054082 *VB 34*

Fernando DE LUCIA (t) Maria GALVANY (s)

La Sonnambula : Prendi l'anel ti dono (Bellini)

(1443 c) c. - 5-08 G. 054217

IRCC 65 Emmy DESTINN (s)

Rusalka : Lieblicher Mond (Dvorak)

(C 14757-3) 9- 3-15 V. 88519 *VB 24*

Damon (Die Bekehrte) (Engl.) (Stange op.13 No.1)

(C 17497-2) 21- 4-16 V. 88565

IRCC 66 * Ada CROSSLEY (c)

Paysage (Hahn)

(A 2190) 30- 4-03 V. M-2190

Caro mio ben (Giordani)

(A 2186) 30- 4-03 V. M-2186

* These two titles are from Fagan & Moran's *Encyclopedic Discography* of *Victor Records Vol. 1* Listing of Pre-matrix numbers. Volume two gives the same two items plus A 2189 *'Four-Leaf Clover'* (Crossley) - all three marked as IRCC 66.

IRCC 67 Geraldine FARRAR (s)

La Recontre Imprévue : Wonnevoller Mai (Un riusselet bien clair) (Gluck)

(B 12740-1) 19-12-12 V. 87127

(IRCC 67 rr) *Le Nozze di Figaro : Non so più cosa son* (Mozart)

(BVE 37351-1) 12- 1-27 V. Unp. 1st. Issue

IRCC 68 Geraldine FARRAR (s)

Le Nozze di Figaro : Voi che sapete (Mozart)

(C 6655-1) 8-12-08 V. 88145

Don Giovanni : Batti, batti, o bel Masetto (Mozart)

(C 6064-1) 30- 3-08 V. 88126

IRCC 69 Zelie DE LUSSAN (s)

Lili (Lola mine) (Guétary)

(A 2187 - B16-1)* 17- 5-03 V. M-2187 *AGSA 33*

Rosy Morn (Ronald)
(A 2199 - B 20-1)* 17- 5-03 V. M-2199
* 'A' matrices re-numbered as 'B' - both versions shown.

IRCC 70 Lucrezia BORI (s)
Iris : Un dì, ero piccina, al tempio (Mascagni)
(C 15824-2) 23- 3-15 V. 88524
Il Segreto di Susanna : O gioia la nube (Wolf-Ferrari)
(B 25301-9) 23-11-21 V. 88647

IRCC 72 Emilio DE GOGORZA (b) (as Carlos Francisco)
Faust : Là, sul campo .. Dio possente (Avant de quitter) (Gounod)
(B 417-2) 15- 9-03 V. 437
Emilio DE GOGORZA (b)
Voici que le printemps (Debussy)
(BVE 43617-1) 6- 4-28 V. Unp. 1st. Issue

IRCC 73 Jeanne GERVILLE-RÉACHE (ms)
Paul et Virginie : Parmi les lianes au fond des savanes (Massé)
(C 9700-2) 5- 5-11 V. 88317 *V. 15- 1008*
La Reine de Saba : Plus grand, dans son obscurité (Gounod)
(C 8332-1) 29-10-09 V. Unp. 1st. Issue

IRCC 74 Olive FREMSTAD (s)
ss *Tosca : Vissi d'arte* (Puccini)
(30644-1) 21- 1-11 Col.A.5282 *AF 2*

IRCC 75 Antonio SCOTTI (b)
Don Pasquale : Bella siccome un angelo (Donizetti)
(B 1092-1) 10- 3 04 V. 81043
Un Ballo in Maschera : Alla vita che t'arride (Verdi)
(B 2360-1) 2- 3-05 V. 81070

IRCC 76 Emma EAMES (s)
Chérubin : Viva amour (Aubade) (Massenet)
Si tu le veux (Massenet)
(C 6202) 18- 5-08 V. 88135
Gretchen am Spinrade (Schumann)
(C 11312) 28-11-11 V. 88367 *AGSB 22*

IRCC 77 Mattia BATTISTINI (b)
Il Barbiere di Siviglia : Largo al factotum (Rossini)
(447 z) 1902 G. 52671 *AGSA 24*

(IRCC 77 rr) Eugenia MANTELLI (c)
La Cenerentola : Non più mesta (Rossini)
(6553) 1907 U.S. Zono.12614

IRCC 78 Bessie ABOTT (s)
Mignon : Io son Titania (Je suis Titania) (Thomas)
(C 6237-1) 27- 5-08 V. 88171
Mario ANCONA (b) Bessie ABOTT (s)

Rigoletto : Tutte le feste al tempio ... Piangi fanciulla (Verdi)
(C 4991-2) 6- 1-08 V. Unp. 1st. Issue

IRCC 79 Geraldine FARRAR (s)
J'ai tant de choses à vous dire (Ferrari)
(B 26869-1) 8- 9-22 V. Unp. 1st. Issue

(IRCC 79 rr) *Opernball : Midnight Bells* (E) (Heuberger)
(BVE 37354-2) 13- 1-27 V. Unp. 1st. Issue

IRCC 80 Sigrid ARNOLDSON (s)
La Traviata : Ah fors' è lui (Verdi)
(1298 r) 1905 G. 53467
Manon : N'est-ce plus ma main (Massenet)
(10848 L) 6- 5-10 G. 33844

IRCC 81 Pol PLANÇON (bs)
L' Étoile du Nord : Ô jours heureux (Meyerbeer)
(C 6111-1) 14- 4-08 V. 85124
Stabat Mater : Pro peccatis (Rossini)
(C 6113-1) 14- 4-08 V. Unp. 1st. Issue
AGSB 74

IRCC 82 Emmy DESTINN (s)
Der Fliegende Holländer : Traft ihr das Schiff (Wagner)
(514 i) 1906 G. 043064
Le Nozze di Figaro : Aria de Grafin (Dove sono) (Mozart)
(0802 v) 1908 G. 043096

IRCC 84 Celestina BONINSEGNA (s)
Loreley: Lascia per or che libera (Catalani)
(3197 c) 2- 6-17 G. 2-053136
Celestina BONINSEGNA (s) & Luigi BOLIS (t)
Il Guarany: Pery ! Che brami ? ... Sento una forza indomita (Gomez)
(3198 c) 2- 6-17 G. 2-054087

IRCC 86 Giuseppe CAMPANARI (b)
L'Africaine : All'erta marinar ...Adamastor, rè dell'onde profonde (Adamastor, roi des vagues) (Meyerbeer)
(C 742-1) 23-11-03 V. 85027
Un Ballo in Maschera : Eri tu (Verdi)
(C 431-1) 18- 9-03 V. 85001

IRCC 87 Lillian NORDICA (s)
Hunyadi László: Ah rebegès, a mi vadúl (Erkel)
(30144-1) 23- 5-07 Col. 68080-D
Ständchen (R. Strauss)
(30677-1) 16- 2-11 Col. 30677

IRCC 89 Blanche MARCHESI (s)
Dido & Aeneas : When I am laid in earth (Purcell)
(TTP 853-2) 1936 Private Issue

Sicilian Cart Driver's Song (arr. Sadero)
(TTP 854-1) 1936 Private Issue

IRCC 90 Emma EAMES (s)
Cavalleria Rusticana : Voi lo sapete (Mascagni)
(C 4034-2) * 16-11-06 V. 88037

* Both this and the earlier version (C 3388-2 dd.14- 5-06) are given in Fagan / Moran as issued on this same IRCC number - it may be relevant that the later version was issued on G. 053092 according to Kelly's *'La Voce del Padrone'*.

Chanson des baisers (Bemberg)
(C 6206-1) 19- 5-08 V. 88133 *AGSB 5*

IRCC 91 Melanie KURT (s)
Die Walküre : Der Männer Sippe (Wagner)
(2390 c) 13- 9-11 G. 043190
Melanie KURT (s) Jacques URLUS (t) Paul KNÜPFER (bs)
Fidelio : Euch werde Lohn (Beethoven)
(606 m) 13- 3-12 G. 044203

IRCC 92 Maria GALVANY (s)
Linda di Chamounix: O luce di quest'anima (Donizetti)
(11190 b) 1908 G. 53549
Fado Portuguez : Ouvi dizar (Neupatk)
(11187½ b) 1908 G. 53558

IRCC 93 Ernestine SCHUMANN-HEINK (c)
Le Prophète : Scène de la prison (1) *(Ô Prêtres de Baal)* (Meyerbeer)
(C 4838-2) 26- 9-07 V. 88094 *AGSB 17*
Sapho : Ô ma lyre immortelle (Gounod)
(C 8232-1) 17- 9-09 V. 88212

The 'Sapho' aria is given on an IRCC dealer's listing. Fagan / Moran give this second side as :
Le Prophète : Scène de la prison (2) *(Il va venir)* (Meyerbeer)
(C 4839-1) 26- 9-07 V. 88095 *AGSB 17*

** To confuse one even more, the IRCC list says "Prison Scene part 2 V. 88094"

IRCC 94 Pol PLANÇON (bs)
Mignon : Berceuse (It) *(De son coeur j'ai calmé la fièvre)* (Thomas)
(C 6112-2) 14- 4-08 V. 85126 *AGSB 74*

Le Lazzarone (Ferrari)
Le Filibustier (Georges)
(C 2323-1) 20- 2-05 V. 85066 *V. 15- 1007*

(IRCC 95 rr) Lillian NORDICA (s)
ss *Die Walküre : Ho-Yo To-Ho* (Wagner)
(Col.Test 30659) 3- 2-11 Col. Unp. 1st. Issue

IRCC 96 John McCORMACK (t)
La Traviata : Lunge da lei ... De' miei bollenti spiriti (Verdi)

(C 8693-1) 10- 3-10 V. Unp. G. 2-052025 *AGSB 3*

John McCORMACK (t) Mario SAMMARCO (b)
Il Barbiere di Siviglia : O, il meglio di scordavo ! (Rossini)
(5205 f) 18- 7-11 G. 2-054021 *VB33*

(IRCC 97 rr) Blanche MARCHESI (s)
L'Eté (Chaminade)
(4132 h) 1906 G. 33593

IRCC 97
Queen Anne Boleyn in Prison (arr.Dolmetch)
(TTP 1166-1) 1936 Private Issue

IRCC 98 Suzanne ADAMS (s)
Coquette (Stern)
(G 2036 FG) 1902 G. 3292
Roméo et Juliette : Valse : (Je veux vivre dans ce rêve) (Gounod)
(G 2037 nB) 1902 G. 3293

IRCC 99 Leo SLEZAK (t)
Die Königin von Saba : Magische Töne (Goldmark)
(14585 u) - 5-09 G. 4-42361 *VA 22*
La Dame Blanche : Komm, o holde Dame
(*Viens, gentille dame*) (Boieldieu)
(690 r) 1905 G. 3-42460 *VA 3*

IRCC 102 Pol PLANÇON (bs)
La Vallon (Gounod)
(C 2319-1) 20- 2-05 V. 85064

Charles GILIBERT (b)
Bergerette (Weckerlin)
Margot s'en va t'en Guerre (Old French folksong)
(C 4364-1) 1- 4-07 V. 85120

IRCC 103 Louise HOMER (ms)
Le Prophète : Ô toi qui m'abbandonnes (Meyerbeer)
(C 491-1) 5-10-03 V. 85004
Adriana Lecouvreur : Acerbe voluttà (Cilea)
(C 3934-1) 24- 1-06 V. 85110

IRCC 104 Fernando DE LUCIA (t) Josefina HUGUET (s)
Lohengrin : Mio salvatore ... Mai devi domandarmi (Mein Held, mein Retter .... Nie sollst du mich brefagen) (Wagner)
(1171 c) 7- 9-07 G. 054175

Fernando DE LUCIA (t) Maria GALVANY (s)
La Sonnambula : Son geloso (Bellini)
(1444 c) c. - 5-08 G. 054215

IRCC 105 Eva GAUTHIER (s)
Le Pré aux Clercs : Souvenirs de jeune age (Hérold)

(B 28858-2) 1916 V. 69223
Fantoches (Debussy)
Romance (Debussy)
(B 20144-1) 20- 6-17 V. 69669

IRCC 108 Mario ANCONA (b)
La Favorite : A tanto amor (Pour tant d'amour) (Donizetti)
(C 4286-2 (3)) 3- 4-07 V. 88063
Dinorah : Sei vendicata assai (Ah ! mon remords te venge) (Meyerbeer)
(C 6044-1) 20- 3-08 V. 88169

IRCC 109 Jeanne GERVILLE-RÉACHE (ms)
Chanson Slave (Chaminade)
(B 8336-1) 30-10-09 V. 87035
Werther : Va ! laisse-les couler mes larmes (Massenet)
(B 7022-2) 29- 4-09 V. 81091 *AGSA 1*

(IRCC 110 rr) Jean DE RESZKE (t)
L'Africaine : ... salut ! Monde nouveau (Ô paradis) (Pt.2) (Meyerbeer)
15- 3-01 Mapleson Cylinder
Andreas DIPPEL * (t) Adolf von HUBBENET (t)
Siegfried : Ho-ho, Ho-hei (Wagner)
* Originally listed as De Reszke not known Mapleson Cylinder

IRCC 111 Frances ALDA (s)
Falstaff: Sul fil d'un soffio etesio (Verdi)
(C 8883-1) 25- 4-10 V. 88247 *AGSB 16*
Loreley: Ah dunque (Catalani)
(C 11150) 4- 4-12 V. 88325

IRCC 113 Emma EAMES (s) Emilio DE GOGORZA (b)
Il Trovatore : Mira d'acerbe lagrime (Verdi)
(C 6233-5) 7 - 4-09 V. 89022 *AGSB 15*
Emilio DE GOGORZA (b)
Rigoletto : Pari siamo (Verdi)
(C 7066-1) 12- 5-09 V. 74110

IRCC 114 Geraldine FARRAR (s)
Le Donne Curiose : Ah, tutta per te, mio bene (Wolf-Ferrari)
(C 11608-2) 21- 2-12 V. 88356
Roméo et Juliette : Valse (Je veux vivre dans ce rêve) (Gounod)
(C 9855-1) 26- 1-11 V. Unp. 1st. Issue
AGSB 55

IRCC 115 Robert BLASS (bs)
Parsifal : Charfreitagszauber (Du sieh'st, ist nicht so) (Wagner)
(C 584-1) 19-10-03 V. 85009
Dichterliebe No.1 *Wunderschönen Monat Mai*
Dichterliebe No.7 *Ich grolle nicht* (Schumann Op.48)
(C 580-1) 16-10-03 V. 85011

IRCC 116 Luisa TETRAZZINI (s)
La Traviata : Addio del passato (Verdi)
(HO 519 af) 26- 9-13 G. 2-053096
I Puritani : Vien diletto (Bellini)
(HO 193 ac) 10- 7-12 G. 2-053072

IRCC 117 Ellison VAN HOOSE (t)
Aïda : Celeste Aïda (Verdi)
(C 3016) * 18- 1-06 V. 74007
* Two takes made this date - both Issued.
Riccardo MARTIN (t)
Cavalleria Rusticana : Ma, prima voglio (Mamma quel vino) (Mascagni)
(C 9696-1) 8-12-10 V. 88277
V. 15-1029

IRCC 119 Blanche MARCHESI (s)
Nun wandre Maria (Wolf)
La Lettre (Moret)
(TPX 5377-1) 1937 Private Issue
Hercules : Air : My father! (Handel)
(TPX 5376-1) 21-12-37 Private Issue

IRCC 120 Margerethe MATZENAUER (ms)
Die Walküre : Nicht weise bin ich (Wagner)
(392½ s) 1909 G. 043129
L'Africaine : In grembo a me (Sour mes genoux) (Meyerbeer)
(C 11689-1) 8- 3-12 V. 88360

IRCC 121 Johanna GADSKI (s)
Tannhäuser : Verzheit wenn ich (Wagner)
(C 13181-2) 23- 4-13 V. 88442
Tannhäuser : Zurück von ihm (Wagner)
(C 13182-2) 23- 4-13 V. 88443

IRCC 122 Sigrid ARNOLDSON (s)
Carmen : Près de ramparts de Séville (Bizet)
(1285 r) - 6-06 G. 33609
Faust : Il était un roi de Thulé (Gounod)
(12486 u) - 3-08 G. 33704

IRCC 123 Dame Nellie MELBA (s)
Sur le lac (Bemberg)
(520 c) 4- 9-05 G. 03046
Nymphs et Sylvains (Bemberg)
(Melba 2) - 3-04 G. 03016

IRCC 124 Melanie KURT (s) & Ottilie METZGER (c)
Le Prophète : Nein, so dank der Hoffnung (Meyerbeer)
(2168 c) 20- 1-11 G. 044176
Melanie KURT (s) Margerethe MATZENAUER (ms)

Le Prophète : Ein armer pilger naht (Un pauvre pélerin) (Meyerbeer)
(2118 c) 7- 12-10 G. 044175

IRCC 125 Emma EAMES (s)
Otello : Ave Maria (Verdi)
(C 3385-2) 14- 5-06 V. 88035
L'Incrédule (Hahn)
Year's at the Spring (Beach)
(C 2314 -2) 16-3-05 V. 85057

IRCC 126 Rosa PONSELLE (s) Giovanni MARTINELLI (t)
Aïda : Pur ti riveggo (Verdi)
(C 29446-2) 7- 2-24 V. Unp. 1st. Issue
VB.73
Rosa PONSELLE (s)
Old folks at home (Foster)
(CVE 32865-4) 4- 6-25 V. Unp. G. DB.872

IRCC 127 Eva GAUTHIER (s)
Le retour des' promis (Dessauer)
(B 19277-2) 14- 3-17 G. 7-33047

(IRCC 127 rr) *Nina Boboh* (Malaysian song arr: Seelig) *
* Said to be from an Unpublished 1915 Columbia - Not traced.

IRCC 128 Johanna GADSKI (s)
Götterdämmerung : Zu neuen Taten (Wagner)
(B 8599-3) 14- 3-12 V. 87098
Götterdämmerung : Betrug ! Schändlichster Betrug ! (Wagner)
(B 8924 2) 7- 5-10 V. Unp. 1st. Issue

IRCC 129 Marcella SEMBRICH (s)
Halka : Gydyby rannem slonkiem (Moniuszko)
(C 4860-2) 5-10-07 V. 88101 *AGSB 87*
Si me vers avaient des ailes ! (Hahn)
Die Schöne Müllerin : Wohin ? (Schubert)
(C 5046-1) 30- 1-08 V. Unp. 1st. Issue
AGSB 88

IRCC 130 Mario ANCONA (b)
Andrea Chénier : Un dì m'era di gioia (Giordano)
(C 6045-1) 20- 3-08 V. 88170
Faust : Non val, perchè mai (Ecoute-moi bien) (Gounod)
(C 4992-1) 6- 1-08 V. (88109) Ist.Issue
AGSB 64

IRCC 131 Maurice RENAUD (b)
Rondel de l'adieu (Partir, c'est mourir un peu) (de Lara)
(5716 o) 1906 G. 3-32669
Charles DALMORÈS (t)
Le Prophète : Roi du ciel (Meyerbeer)

(B 4395-3) 25- 3-08 V. Unp. 1st. Issue *AGSA 15*

IRCC 132 Geraldine FARRAR (s)
Roland von Berlin : Fahr wohl ! Trautgesell ! (Leoncavallo)
(2496 L) 1904 G. 43632 *HMB 118*
Dear heart (Mattei)
(3799 h) 27- 9-05 G. 3621

IRCC 133 Pol PLANÇON (bs)
Martha : Chi mi dirà (Porterlied) (Flotow)
(B 4346-1) 27- 3-07 V. 81086 *AGSA 45*
Credo (Fauré)
(B 2339-1) 25- 2 -05 V. 81066

IRCC 138 Edmond CLÉMENT (t) Marcel JOURNET (bs)
Robert le Diable : Du rendezvous (Meyerbeer)
(C 11468-1) 18- 1-12 G. 2-034015 *VB 30*
Robert le Diable : Le bonheur est dans l'inconstance (Meyerbeer)
(C 11469-1) 18- 1-12 G. 2-034016 *VB 30*

IRCC 139 Marcella SEMBRICH (s)
Der Nussbaum (Schumann op.25 No. 3)
(B 1951-3) 19-11-04 V. 81049
Ständchen (R. Strauss)
(B 1950-2) 19-11-04 V. 81048

IRCC 140 Johanna GADSKI (s) Albert REISS (t)
Bartered Bride : Ich weiss Euch einen lieben schatz (Smetana)
(C 7025-1) 30- 4-09 V. Unp. 1st. Issue *AGSB 12*

Albert REISS (t)
Siegfried : Zwangvolle Plage (Wagner)
V. 74235

IRCC 141 Emilio DE GOGORZA (b)
Patrie : Air du Sonneur (Paladilhe)
(C 10997-1) 19- 9-11 V. 74229
Benvenuto Cellini : De l'art splendour immortelle (Diaz)
V. Unp. 1st. Issue

IRCC 142 Celestina BONINSEGNA (s)
Il Trovatore : Tacea la notte placida (Verdi)
(537 c) 1905 G. 053063
L'Africaine : Di qui io veda il mar ... Già l'odio m'abbandona
(D'ici je vois la mer ... La haine m'abbandona) (Meyerbeer)
(535½ c) 1905 G. 053068

IRCC 143 Mattia BATTISTINI (b)
Eugene Onegin : Se dell'imen la dolce cura (Tchaikovsky)
(441 z) 1902 G. 52665

Demon : Deh non plorar (Rubinstein)
(446 z) 1902 G. 52670 *HMB 85*

IRCC 145 Pol PLANÇON (bs)
Die Jahreszeiten : No.5: (Chant du Laboureur) (Haydn)
(C 2321-1) 20- 2-05 V. 85082
Le Cor (Flégier)
(C 2336-1) 25- 2-05 V. 85076

IRCC 146 Johanna GADSKI (s) Otto GORITZ (b)
Der Fliegende Holländer : Versank ich jetzt (Wagner)
(C 11723-1) 14- 3-12 V. 88370
Der Fliegende Holländer : Wohl kenn'ich (Wagner)
(C 11725-2) 14- 3-12 V. 88371

IRCC 147 Louise Kirkby LUNN (c) Emmy DESTINN (s)
La Gioconda : L'amo come il fulgor del creato (Ponchielli)
(5143 f) 6- 7-11 G. 2-054020
Louise Kirkby LUNN (c)
La Clemenza di Tito : Non più di fiori (Mozart)
(z 5500 f) 22- 9-11 G. 2-053068
AGSB 21

IRCC 148 Luisa TETRAZZINI (s)
La Sonnambula : Come per me sereno (Bellini)
(HO 188 ac) 9- 7-12 G. 2-053070
Voce di Primavera (J. Strauss)
(2586 f) - 9-08 G. 053197

IRCC 150 Dame Nellie MELBA (s) (Chorus : Dawson, Pike, G. Roberts)
Come back to Erin (Claribel)
(7202½ c) 4- 9-05 G. 3616
Good-night (Scott - Gatty)
(7204 b) 4- 9-05 G. 3618

IRCC 151 Margerethe SIEMS (s)
Der Rosenkavalier : Kann mich auch an ein Mädel erinnern (R. Strauss)
(2303 c) 25- 8-11 G. 043179
Minnie NASTS Eva Plaschke VON DER OSTEN (s)
Der Rosenkavalier : Ist ein Traum (R. Strauss)
(2304 c) 25- 8-11 G. 044183

IRCC 152 David BISPHAM (b)
O that we two were maying (Gounod)
(268 R (c)) 20- 8-03 G. 02046
Tannhäuser : Als du im kühnem Sange (Wagner)
(WG 266 R (c)) 20- 8-03 G. 042050

IRCC 153 Louise HOMER (ms)
Orphée et Eurydice : Away with mourning and crying (Gluck)
(C 622-1) 2-11-03 V. 85015

Alceste : Fatal divinita (Divinités du Styx) (Gluck)
V. 88286

(IRCC 154 rr) Lillian NORDICA (s) Georg ANTHES (t)
Siegfried : fragments Act 3 duo 'O Siegfried' (Wagner)
19- 1-03 Mapleson Cylinder
Siegfried : Finale of Opera (Wagner)
19- 1-03 Mapleson Cylinder
Lillian NORDICA (s)
Götterdämmerung : Immolation not known Mapleson Cylinder

(IRCC 155 rr) Lillian NORDICA (s)
ss *Götterdämmerung : Immolation* not known Mapleson Cylinder *
* Different performance to 154

IRCC 156 Geraldine FARRAR (s)
Nymphes et Faunes (Sylvains) (Bemberg)
(C 6063-1) 30- 3-08 V. Unp ? [V. 88125 ?]
Tosca : Ora stammi a sentir (Puccini)
(C 9834-2) 26- 1-11 V. 88287

IRCC 157 Pol PLANÇON (bs)
Embarques-vous (Godard)
(B 1052-1) 27- 2-04 V. 81039
Si tu veux, Mignonne (Massenet)
(B 2320-1) 20- 2-05 V. 81076

(IRCC 159 rr) Susan STRONG (s)
Herodiade : Il est doux, il est bon (Massenet)
(2435 f) 11- 9-08 G. 03116

IRCC 159 *Die Junge Nonne* (Schubert)
(2004 f) 1907 G. 043078 *VB 13*

IRCC 160 NOT USED

IRCC 161 Frieda HEMPEL (s)
Lakmé : Bell song (Où va la jeune Hindoue) (Delibes)
(2411 c) 15- 9-11 G. 033144
Der Wildschutz : Auf des Lebens (Lortzing)
(1174 s) 18- 9-13 G. 043247 *AGSB 59*

(IRCC 162 rr) Mme. Charles CAHIER (c)
Le Prophète : Ah ! mon fils (Meyerbeer
(CS 2946-1T1) 20- 9-28 G. M.109 *HMB 69*

IRCC 162 *La Favorite : Ô mon Fernando* (Donizetti)
(CS 2947-2) 20- 9-28 G. M.109 *HMB 69*

(IRCC 163 rr) Emma CALVÉ (s) Emilio DE MARCHI (t)
Carrie BRIDEWELL (ms) Giuseppe CAMPANARI (b)
Cavalleria Rusticana (fragments) : Battimi, Insultami /
Ah ! No ! Turiddu (Mascagni)
22- 2-02 Mapleson Cylinder
Emma CALVÉ (s) Marcel JOURNET (bs) Andreas DIPPEL (t)

Faust fragments : Jewel Song (last half) / *Final Trio* (Gounod)
15- 2-02 Mapleson Cylinder

IRCC 164 Johanna GADSKI (s)
Oberon : Ozean, du Ungeheuer (Ocean, thy mighty monster) (1) (Weber)
(C 13183-1) 6- 5-14 V. 88495
Oberon : Ozean, du Ungeheuer (Ocean, thy mighty monster) (2) (Weber)
(C 14804-5) 15- 6-15 V. 88545

IRCC 165 Selma KURZ (s)
An dem schönen blauen Donau (J.Strauss)
(Cc 6973 -2) 15-10-25 G. 2-043045 *VB 35*
Le Nozze di Figaro : Deh vieni, non tardar (Mozart)
(Cc 6992 -2A) 16-10-25 G. 2-053250 *VB 35*

(IRCC 167rr) Lillian NORDICA (s) Ernestine SCHUMANN-HEINK (c)
2ss Georg ANTHES (t)
Tristan und Isolde : (3 Fragments) *Love duet* (Wagner)
9- 2-03 Mapleson Cylinder

(IRCC 168 rr) Johanna GADSKI (s) Edouard DE RESZKE (bs)
2ss *Les Huguenots : Marcel-Valentine duet* Act 3 (4 fragments) (Meyerbeer)
24- 1-03 Mapleson Cylinder

IRCC 169 Charles DALMORÈS (t) Marcel JOURNET (bs
Carmen : Je suis Escamillo (Bizet)
(C 4253-1) 19- 2-07 V. 85114 *AGSB 19*
Faust : Ô Merveille (Gounod)
(C 4254-1) 19- 2-07 V. 85115 *AGSB 19*

(IRCC 170 rr) Marcella SEMBRICH (s) Thomas SALIGNAC (t)
La Fille du Regiment : Duetto Act 1 (De cet aveu si tendre) (Donizetti)
30- 1-03 Mapleson Cylinder
Marcella SEMBRICH (s) Thomas SALIGNAC (t)
Charles GILIBERT (b) Marie VAN CAUTEREN (s)
La Fille du Regiment : En avant, Rataplan ! (Donizetti)
30- 1-03 Mapleson Cylinder
Fritzi SCHEFF (s) Thomas SALIGNAC (t)
Marcel JOURNET (bs)
Faust : Il m'aime (to end of scene) (Gounod)
14- 2-03 Mapleson Cylinder

IRCC 171 Julia CULP (c)
Feldeinsamkeit (Brahms)
(BW 158-1) 21- 8-26 Electrola EW 9
Du bist wie eine Blume (Schumann op.25 No.4)
(BW 157-3) 21- 8-26 Electrola EW 9

IRCC 172 Leo SLEZAK (t)
Guillaume Tell : O Matilde (Ah, Mathilde, je t'aime) (Rossini)
(820 z) 1903 G. 2-42592

Francesco TAMAGNO (t)
Hérodiade : Adieu vains objets (Massenet)
(3016 FT) - 2-03 G. 52680

IRCC 174 Florence EASTON (s)
Hat dich die Liebe berührt (Marx)
(0B 5561-1) 18- 1-34 G. Unp. Ist.Issue *HMA 131*
Songs my mother taught me (Dvorak)
(0B 5558-1) 18- 1-34 G. Unp. Ist.Issue *HMA 131*

(IRCC 177 rr) Lillian NORDICA (s) Johanna GADSKI (s) Louise HOMER (ms)
Ernestine SCHUMANN-HEINK (ms)
Mathilde BAUERMEISTER (s) Marie VAN CAUTEREN (s)
Camille SEYGARD (s) Marguerite MARILLY (s)
Carrie BRIDEWELL (ms) Marie MAURER (ms)
Die Walküre : fragment *'Herlichste Maid !'* (Wagner)
21- 2-03 Mapleson Cylinder
Louise HOMER (ms) Ernestine SCHUMANN-HEINK (ms)
Mathilde BAUERMEISTER (s) Marie VAN CAUTEREN (s)
Camille SEYGARD (s) Marguerite MARILLY (s)
Carrie BRIDEWELL (ms) Marie MAURER (ms)
Die Walküre : Ride of the Walküres (Wagner) (Two fragments)
21- 2-03 Mapleson Cylinder

(IRCC 179 rr) Emma EAMES (s) Emilio DE MARCHI (t) Antonio SCOTTI (b)
Tosca : Ah mostro (Puccini) 3- 3-03 Mapleson Cylinder
Emma EAMES (s) Emilio DE MARCHI (t) Antonio SCOTTI (b)
Tosca : Vittoria ! (Puccini) 3- 3-03 Mapleson Cylinder

IRCC 180 Olimpia BORONAT (s)
Les Pêcheurs de Perles : Siccome un dì
(*Comme autrefois dans la nuit*) (Bizet)
(1777 L) 1904 G. 53353 *VA 11*
Rigoletto : Caro nome (Verdi)
(1772 L) 1904 G. 53348

IRCC 181 Dame Nellie MELBA (s)
Three green bonnets (d'Hardelot)
(Melba 25) - 3-04 G. 03027
Spring (Henschel)
(4213 f) - 5-10 G. 03328

(IRCC 183 rr) Jean DE RESZKE (t)
L'Africaine : Ô paradis (two fragments) (Meyerbeer)
Lucienne BREVAL Jean DE RESZKE (t)
L'Africaine : Duet Act 4 (three fragments) (Meyerbeer)
15- 3-01 Mapleson Cylinder

Lohengrin : Mein Herr und Konig (Wagner)
29- 3-01 Mapleson Cylinder

IRCC 184 Emmy DESTINN (s)
Tannhäuser : Dich, teure Halle (Wagner)
(272 ac) 18-10-09 G. 043133
Dalibor : Wär'es Wahr ? (Jak je mi ?) (Smetana)
(273 ac) 18-10-09 G. 043138

IRCC 185 Pol PLANÇON (bs) *AGSB 12*
Faust : Je ferais de mon moeux ... Le veau d'or (Gounod)
(B 1051-2) 24- 1-05 V. 81038
La Damnation de Faust : Sérénade (Devant la maison) (Berlioz)
(B 874-2) 29- 1-04 V. 81034

IRCC 186 Johanna GADSKI (s)
Die Zauberflöte : Ah, lo so (Ach, ich fühls) (Mozart)
(C 9492-1) 29- 9-10 V. 88254
Tannhäuser : Allmächt'ge Jungfrau (Wagner)
(C 4129-2) 8-12-06 (V. 88044)
1st. Issue.

IRCC 188 Dinh GILLY (b)
O del mio amato ben (Donaudy)
(Cc 14229-4) 16- 1-29 G. 2-052400
Amaryllis (Caccini)
(Cc 14231-1) 15- 8-28 G. 2-052382

IRCC 190 Antonio SCOTTI (b)
Don Carlos : Convien qui dirci ... Per me giunto
(Il faut dire adieu ! ... C'est mon jour suprême) (Verdi)
(C 2359-1) 2- 3-05 V. 85067
L'Elisir d'Amore : Come Paride vezzoso (Donizetti)
(C 2361-1) 2- 3-05 V. 85068 *AGSB 24*

IRCC 193 Francesco TAMAGNO (t)
Otello : Ora e per sempre, addio (Verdi)
(3004 b) 1903 G. 52675

(IRCC 193 rr) Victor MAUREL (b)
Otello : Era la notte (Verdi)
(1632 F) 1904 G. 2-32814

IRCC 194 Emma EAMES (s)
Love in May (Parker)
I once had a dear little doll, dears (Nevin)
(C 6201) 18- 5-08 V. 88131
Spring (Henschel)
Year's at the Spring (Beach)
(C 6203-1) 18- 5-08 V. 88008
AGSB 22

IRCC 195 Geraldine FARRAR (s)
Ring of Haround Al Rashid : Love's like a summer (Chadwick)
(C 12738-1) 19-12-12 V. 88409
My mother bids me bind my hair (Haydn)
(C 9835-1) 23- 1-11 V. 88289
IRCC 197 Maria GAY (c)
Don Giovanni : Vedrai carino (Mozart)
(3807 f) 8-11-09 G. 2-053016
Carmen : Les tringles des sistres tintaient (Bizet)
(3816 f) 9-11-09 G. 2-063000
(IRCC 201 rr) Johanna GADSKI (s) Luise REUSS-BELCE (s)
Lohengrin : Duo Elsa-Ortrud (...wohl bewahrt) (Wagner)
7- 2-03 Mapleson Cylinder
Johanna GADSKI (s) Georg ANTHES (t)
Lohengrin : Mein Held ... (Wagner)
7- 2-03 Mapleson Cylinder
IRCC 202 Mattia BATTISTINI (b)
Zampa : Perchè tremar ? (Hérold)
(889 c) -11-06 G. 052148 *AGSB 52*
Macbeth : Perfidi ... Pietà, rispetto, amore (Verdi)
(234 af) 30- 5-12 G. 052369 *ABHB 4*
IRCC 203 Rosa RAISA (s)
La Gioconda : Suicidio (Ponchielli)
(2M 1445) 30- 6-33 G. DB.2122
Cavalleria Rusticana : Voi lo sapete (Mascagni)
(2M 1446) 30- 6-33 G. DB.2123
IRCC 208 Elena GERHARDT (ms)
Wie sollten wir (R.Strauss)
Neue Liebe (Rubinstein)
(3540 r) 1907 G. 2-43181
Ich hab'ein kleines Lied erdacht (Bungert)
(3539 r) 1907 G. 2-43180
IRCC 215 Geraldine FARRAR (s)
Caro mio ben (Giordani)
(3801 h) 27- 9-05 G. 53430
Liebe Augustin : Der Himmel Hängt (Walz song) (Fall)
(B 12951-1)
27- 2-13 V. 87134
(IRCC 216 rr) Jean DE RESZKE (t) Milka TERNINA (s)
Tristan und Isolde : Love Duet (3 fragments) (Wagner) :
9- 2-03 Mapleson Cylinder
Emma EAMES (s)
Tosca : Finale (Puccini) 3- 3-03 Mapleson Cylinder

	Milka TERNINA (s)		
	Tosca : Finale (Puccini)	not known	Mapleson Cylinder
IRCC 217	John McCORMACK (t)		
	Sospiri miei andate ove vi mando (Bimboni)		
	(B 13032-1)	28- 3-13	V. 64333 *VA 20*
	O del mio amato ben (Donaudy)		
	(Bb 5035-1)	4- 9-24	G. 7-52276 *AGSA 49*
(IRCC 219 rr)	Lillian NORDICA (s)		
	Die Walküre : Beginning of 'Ho-jo-to-ho' (Wagner)		
		21- 2-03	Mapleson Cylinder
	Tristan & Isolde : Liebestod Fragment (Wagner)		
		9- 2-03	Mapleson Cylinder
(IRCC 232rr)	Lillian NORDICA (s)		
	La Gioconda : Suicidio (Ponchielli)		
	(30133-1)	3- 4-06	Col. Unp. 1st. Issue
	(from Test pressings)		
	Il Trovatore : Tacea la notte (Verdi)		
	(C.30134-1)	3- 4-06	Col. Unp. 1st. Issue
	(from Test pressings)		
(IRCC 237 rr)	Lillian NORDICA (s) Marcello RESENINIL (?) (t)		
	Il Trovatore : Miserere (Verdi)		
	(30137-2)	3- 4-06	Col. Unp. 1st. Issue
	Ada ADINI (s)		
	Il Trovatore : D'amore sull'ali rosee (Verdi)		
	(XXPh) not known	F. 39112	
IRCC 5001	Fernando DE LUCIA (t)		
	Serenamente (Barthélemy)		
	(13334 b)_	21- 5-09	G. 2-52772 *HMA 2*
	Sulla bocca amorosa (Barthélemy)		
	(13331 b)	21- 5-09	G. 2-52698
(IRCC 5002 rr)*	* The identification of the singer and date of performance are debatable and a definitive date unknown. The singers suggested are Melba OR Adams though the former was named on the issued disc.		
	Les Huguenots : A ce mot(Meyerbeer)		
			Mapleson Cylinder
IRCC 5003	Fernando DE LUCIA (t)		
	Era di maggio (Costa)		
	(13332 b)	21- 5-09	G. 2-52699
	Ideale (Tosti)		
	(2861 b)	-11-02	G. 52410
IRCC 5008 (rr?)	Eugenia MANTELLI (ms)		

La Gioconda : Voce di donna (Ponchielli)
Zono. 12586
Faust : La parlate d'amor (Faites-lui mes aveux) (Gounod)
Zono. 12617

HISTORIC RECORD SOCIETY

HRS 1001 Charles DALMORÈS (t)
Il Trovatore : Ah ! sì ben mio (Verdi)
(C 4394-1) 12- 4-07 V. 85123 *AGSB 9*
Antonio PAOLI (t)
Il Trovatore : Di quella pira (Verdi)
(1182 c) 1907 G. 052170
HRS 1002 Pasquale AMATO (b) Ch
L'Africaine : Adamastor, rè dell'onde profonde (Adamastor, roi des vagues) (Meyerbeer)
(C 14719-2) 16- 4-14 V. 88490
Riccardo MARTIN (t)
Le Cid : Ah ! tout est bien fini ! ... Ô Souverain ! ô Juge ! ô Père (Massenet)
(C 9695-1) 8-12-10 V. 88316 *V. 15-1029*
HRS 1003 Mario ANCONA (b) & Marcel JOURNET (bs)
I Puritani : Suoni la tromba (Bellini)
(C 4285-2) 6- 3-07 V. 88500
Carlo ALBANI (t)
Lucrezia Borgia : Di pescator ignobile (Donizetti)
(C 4887-1) 18-10-07 V. 74098 *AGSB 65*
HRS 1004 Jeanne GERVILLE-RÉACHE (ms)
L'Enfant Prodigue : L'année en vain chasse l'année (Debussy)
(C 9701-3) 5- 5-11 V. 88281
Orphée et Eurydice : J'ai perdu mon Eurydice (Gluck)
(C 7023-1) 29- 4-09 V. 88198
HRS 1005 Marcella SEMBRICH (s) Mario SAMMARCO (b)
Rigoletto : Tutte le feste ... Piangi fanciulla ... Sì vendetta (Verdi)
(C 8755-2) 26- 3-10 V. 89042
Mario SAMMARCO (b)
Rigoletto : Cortigiani, vil razza, dannata (Verdi)
(C 10095-1) 23- 3-11 V. 88315
HRS 1006 Emilio DE GOGORZA (b)
Il Barbiere di Siviglia : Largo al factotum (Rossini)
(B 2190-3) 1- 2-05 V. 4327
Louise HOMER (ms) Emilio DE GOGORZA (b)

Samson et Dalila : Vengeance at last
(A moi l'honneur de la vengeance) (Saint-Saëns)
1907 V. 87501

HRS 1007 Mattia BATTISTINI (b)
Don Giovanni : Finch' han dal vino (Mozart)
(439 z) 1902 G. 52663 *AGSA 24*
Maurice RENAUD (b)
Guillaume Tell : Sois immobile (Rossini)
(5731 o) 1906 G. 3-32671

HRS 1008 Johanna GADSKI (s)
Salome : Jochanaan, ich bin verliebt (R.Strauss)
(C 7030-1) 30- 4-09 V. 81089
Johanna GADSKI (s) & Otto GORITZ (b)
Die Zauberflöte : Papagena ... Papageno (Mozart)
(B 13132-1) 16- 4-13 V. 87510

HRS 1009 Antonio PAOLI (t)
Otello : Dio ! mi potevi scagliar (Verdi)
(1260 c) 1907 G. 052173
Otello : Niun mi tema (Verdi)
(313 aj) 27- 6-11 G. 052328

HRS 1010 Maria GALVANY (s)
Hamlet : Ballata di Ofelia : Ora a noi (A vos jeux, mes amis) (Thomas)
(1307 c) 1907 G. 053162
Dinorah : Ombra leggiera (Ombre légère) (Meyerbeer)
(1451½ c) 1908 G. 053180

HRS 1011 Jeanne GERVILLE-RÉACHE (ms)
D'une prison (Hahn)
(C 10277-1) 5- 5-11 V. 88368
Sapho : Ô ma lyre immortelle (Gounod)
(C 7024-1) 29- 4-09 V. 88166

HRS 1012 Carolina WHITE (c)
ss. *Robert le Diable : Roberto, tu che adoro (Robert, toi que j'aime)*
(Meyerbeer)
(30870-2) 24-10-11 Col. 30870

HRS 1013 NOT ISSUED

HRS 1014 Frances ALDA (s)
Manon Lescaut : L'ora, o Tirsi (Puccini)
(B 10188) 14- 4-11 V. 87079
Manon Lescaut : In quelle trine morbide (Puccini)
(B 11152) 4- 4-12 V. 87106

HRS 1015 Luisa TETRAZZINI (s)
Les Huguenots : O vago suol (Ô beau pays de la Touraine) (Meyerbeer)
(HO 191 ac) 9- 7-12 G. 2-053071

VB 41

Las Hijas del Zebedeo : Carceleras (Al pensar en el dueño) (Chapi)
(C 10057-3) 18- 3-11 V. 88294

HRS 1016 Emma EAMES (s)
Faust : Air des bijoux : Ah ! Je ris de me voir (Gounod)
(C 2317-1) 20- 2-05 V. 85053
Emma EAMES (s) Pol PLANÇON (bs) Charles DALMORÈS (t)
Faust : Alerte ! Alerte ! ou vous êtes perdus (Gounod)
(C 4332-1) 25- 3-07 V. 95300

HRS 1017 Adelina STEHLE (s) Edoardo GARBIN (t)
Adriana Lecouvreur : Ma dunque è vero (Cilea)
(XPh 95) (FD) 23-11-04 F. 39117 *PO 125*
Salomea KRUSCENISCI (s)
Adriana Lecouvreur : Io son l'umile ancella (Cilea)
(XPh 2213) 6-11-06 F. 39922 *PO 132*

HRS 1018 Rosina STORCHIO (s)
Linda di Chamounix : O luce di quest'anima (Donizetti)
(XPh 1502) 2-12-05 F. 39402
Eugenio GIRALDONI (b)
Otello : Era la notte (Verdi)
(XPh 1513) 12-12-05 F. 39445 *HMB 9*

HRS 1019 Rose CARON (s)
Sigurd : Sigurd, les Dieux ... Des présents de Gunther (Reyer)
(XPh 521) * 20-12-04 ? F. 39097
Prière (Gounod)
(XPh 523) * 20-12-04 ? F. 39096

* NOTE : Neither item on Fonotipia Register. Date shown as given on the labels.

HRS 1020 NOT ISSUED

HRS 1021 Pol PLANÇON (bs)
Dinorah (Pardon de Ploermel) : En chasse (Meyerbeer)
(B 2338-1) 25- 2-05 V. 81065
Le Soupir (Bemberg)
(B 2335-1) 25- 2-05 V. 81073

HRS 1022 Alessandro BONCI (t)
Paride ed Elena : O del mio dolce ardor (Gluck)
(XPh 308) 16- 6-05 F. 39241
Alessandro BONCI (t) Regina PINKERT (s)
Don Pasquale : Tornami a dir (Donizetti)
(XPh 438) 8-11-05 F. 39341

HRS 1023 Francesco NAVARINI (bs) (with un-named tenor)
Lucrezia Borgia : Separarsi al alba ... Vieni, la mia vendetta (Donizetti)
(XPh 2397) 1- 2-07 F. 62026 *HMB 83*

Lucrezia Borgia : Qualunque sia l'evento (Donizetti)
(XPh 2398) 1- 2-07 F. 62027 *HMB 83*

HRS 1024 Victor MAUREL (b)
Au temps du grand roi (Tosti)
(XPh 2334) 8- 1-07 F. 62017

Antonio MAGINI-COLETTI (b) Elisa PETRI (s)
Falstaff : Quand'ero paggio (Verdi)
(XPh 1533) 16-12-05 F. 39430

HRS 1025 Fernando DE LUCIA (t)
Carmen : Il fior (La fleur que tu m'avais jetée) (Bizet)
(2899 b) c. 3-12-02 G. 52437 *VA 13*
Lohengrin : Mercè, Cigno gentil (Nun sei bedankt) (Wagner)
(2905 b) c. 3-12-02 G. 52650 *VA 13*

HRS 1026 Helen Beach YAW (s)
Lucia di Lammermoor : Ardon gl'incensi (Donizetti)
(C 4834-1) 25- 9-07 V. Unp. 1st. Issue *AGSB 66*
Le Timbre d'Argent : Le Bonheur est chose légère (Saint-Saëns)
(C 4835-2) 25- 9-07 V. Unp. 1st. Issue *AGSB 202*

HRS 1027 NOT ISSUED

HRS 1028 Jeanne GERVILLE-RÉACHE (ms)
Ich grolle nicht (Schumann)
(B 10278-1) 5- 5-11 V. 87085
Il Trovatore : Stride la vampa (Verdi)
(B 8331-1) 29-10-09 V. 87065

HRS 1029 Eugenia BURZIO (s) Giovanni ZENATELLO (t)
Un Ballo in Maschera : Non sai tu (Verdi)
(XPh 1829) 23- 4-06 F. 39665
Un Ballo in Maschera : O qual soave brivido (Verdi)
(XPh 1830) 23- 4-06 F. 39666

HRS 1030 NOT ISSUED

HRS 1031 Alice NIELSEN (s)
La Fille du Regiment : Convien partir (Donizetti)
not known not known V. 74117

Amelita GALLI-CURCI
Semiramide : Bel raggio lusinghier (Rossini)
(C 30905-2) 16- 9-24 V. Unp. G. 2-053235 *VB 5*

HRS 1033 NOT ISSUED

HRS 1034 Leo SLEZAK (t)
Die Zauberflöte : Bildnisarie (Mozart)
(14578 u) - 5-09 G. 4-42215

Die Entführung aus dem Serail : Hier soll ich dich denn sehen (Mozart)
(10817 u) - 6-07 G. 3-42832

HRS 1035 NOT ISSUED

HRS 1036 Ferruccio CORRADETTI (b)
La Forza del Destino : Urna fatale del mio destino (Verdi)
(XPh 2423) 5- 2-07 F. 62042
Il Barbiere di Siviglia : Manca un foglio (Pietro Romani)
(Inserted into Rossini's opera)
(XPh 459) 14-11-05 F. 39378

HRS 1037 Alma GLUCK (s)
The Czar's Bride : Liuba's aria (G) (Rimsky Korsakov)
(C 14260-3) 14- 2-16 V. 74383
Hippolyte et Aricie : Rossignols amoureux (Rameau)
(C 10811-1) 20- 7-11 V. 74249

(HRS 1038 rr) Fernand ANSSEAU (t)
Samson et Dalila : Vois ma misère (Saint-Saëns)
(CV 178-2T1) 25-10-28 G. DB.1268

HRS 1038 Bernardo DE MURO (t)
Don Carlos : Io l'ho perduto (Je l'ai perdue !) (Verdi)
(744 m) 30- 3-14 G. 052429

HRS 1039 Lucrezia BORI (s) Miguel FLETA (t)
L'Amico Fritz : Tutto tace (Cherry duet Pt.2) (Mascagni)
(C 29285-3) 14- 1-24 V. Unp. 1st. Issue
Carmen : Parle-moi de ma mère (Bizet)
(C 29286-2) 14- 1-24 V. Unp. 1st. Issue
AGSB 58

HRS 1040 NOT ISSUED

HRS 1041 Anton VAN ROOY (b)
Tannhäuser : Lied an den Abendstern (Wagner)
(2498 f) 1908 G. 042167
Carmen : Votre toast (Bizet)
(2501½ f) 1908 G. 032079

HRS 1042 - 1046 NOT ISSUED

HRS 1047 Johanna GADSKI (s)
Lohengrin : Euch Lüften, die mein Klangen (Wagner)
(C 11527-4) 4- 4-12 V. 88377
Wesendonck Lieder No.3 : Im Treibhaus (Wagner)
(C 19688-4) 4- 5-17 V. (88590) 1st. Issue

HRS 1048 - 1052 NOT ISSUED *
* Fagan / Moran lists :

HRS 1049 Bessie ABOTT
Roméo et Juliette : Je veux vivre dans ce rêve (Gounod)
(B 4305-1) 13- 3-07 V. 87007
(Reverse ?)

HRS 1053 Carlo ALBANI (t)

Andrea Chénier : Un dì all'azzuro spazio (Giordano)

(C 4898-1) 28-10-07 V. Unp. 1st. Issue *AGSB 65*

Fernando DE LUCIA (t)

Il Barbiere di Siviglia : Ecco ridente in cielo (Rossini)

(214 m) c. 6-10-04 G. 052078

HRS 1054 Charles DALMORÈS (t)

Samson et Dalila : Arrêtez, ô mes frères !(Saint-Saëns)

(B 11153-2) 1911 V. 87087

Je t'aime (Massenet)

1912 V. 87120

HRS 2001 Fernando DE LUCIA (t)

Tosca : Recondita armonia (Puccini)

(2868 R (b)) c. 30-11-02 G. 52414

Rigoletto : La donna è mobile (Verdi)

(2863 R (b)) c. 30-11-02 G. 52411

HRS 2002 Giuseppe ANSELMI (t)

Manrù : Come al sol cocente (Paderewsky)

(XPh 2845) 8-11-07 F. 62289

Luisa Miller : Ah ! fede negar potessi (Verdi)

(XPh 2836) 8-11-07 F. 62159

HRS 2003 Francesco VIÑAS (t)

Le Prophète : Sopra Berta (Pour Bertha moi je soupire) (Meyerbeer)

(XPh 2102) 2- 2-07 F. 39805

Un Ballo in Maschera : Ma se m' è forza pederti (Verdi)

(XPh 2641) 13- 5-07 F. 62083

HRS 2004 Charles DALMORÈS (t)

Roméo et Juliette : Ah ! lève-toi, soleil (Gounod)

(C 4250-3) 3- 4-07 V. 85121

Griselidis : Ouvrez-vous (Massenet)

(C 12538-1) 25-10-12 V. 88397

HRS 2005 Leo SLEZAK (t)

Le Prophète : Triumphgesang (Roi du ciel) (Meyerbeer)

(6889 b) 1905 G. 3-42376

La Juive : Recha, als Gott dich einst (Rachel, quand du Seigneur)(Halévy)

(689 r) 1905 G. 3-42459

HRS 2006 Riccardo MARTIN (t)

Madama Butterfly : Amore o grillo (Puccini)

(B 9690-1) 7- 3-10 V. 87081

Nicola ZEROLA (t)

Samson et Dalila : Figli miei (Arrêtez, ô mes frères !) (Saint-Saëns)

(B 8492-3) 3- 3-10 V. 64173

HRS 2007 Antonio PAOLI (t)
Les Huguenots : Bianca al par (Plus blanche) (Meyerbeer)
(329 aj) 30- 6-11 G. 052332
Samson et Dalila : Spezzi i ceppi (Saint-Saëns)
(1179 c) 1907 G. 052169

HRS 2008 Léon ESCALAIS (t)
Roberto le Diable : Sicilienne (Meyerbeer)
(XPh 498) 1-12-05 F. 39414
Léon ESCALAIS (t) Oreste LUPPI (bs) Angelo ALGO (t)
Ferruccio CORRADETTI (b) Antonio MAGINI-COLETTI (b)
Giovanni MASOTTI (bs) Giuseppe SALA (t)
Huguenots : Septet (En mon bon droit j'ai confiance !) (Meyerbeer)*
(Xph 473-2) 18-11-05 F. 39370
* Issued both as a direct pressing and as a dubbing under this same number

HRS 2015 Titta RUFFO (b)
La Forza del Destino: Urna fatale (Verdi)
(B 15892-1) 13- 4-15 V. Unp. 1st. Issue
AGSA 10
Il Trovatore : Per me ora fatale (Verdi)
(9217 e) 25-11-08 G. 2-52687

ADDISON FOSTER

AF 1 Rosa PONSELLE (s)
La Juive : Il va venir (Halévy)
(98096-3) * 11- 1-24 Col.Unp. 1st. Issue
Lohengrin : Elsas Traum (Einsam in trüben Tagen) Wagner)
(98093-1) 21- 9-23 Col.Unp. 1st. Issue
* In "*Rosa Ponselle*" (James A.Drake Amadeus Press 1997) Bill Parks' discography shows this as 'take 3 dated 11- 1-24'. *The Columbia Master Book Discography Vol.4* (Rust & Brooks Greenwood Press 1999) shows this Issue number against Takes 3, 4 (without being specific) dated as 10- 6-24.

AF 2 Olive FREMSTAD (s)
Tosca : Vissi d'arte (Puccini)
(30644-1) 21- 1-11 Col. 30644
IRCC 74
Tannhäuser : Dich, teure Halle (Wagner)
(30635-2) 21- 1-11 Col. 30635
IRCC 12

AF 3 Olive FREMSTAD (s)
Lohengrin : Elsas Traum (Einsam in trüben Tagen) (Wagner)
(30645-1) 30- 1-11 Col. 30645

IRCC 12

Lillian NORDICA (s)
Mignon : Je suis Titania (Thomas)
(30661-1) 2- 2-11 Col. 30661

AMERICAN GRAMOPHONE SOCIETY (ADDISON FOSTER) / (HMV)

AGSA 1 Jeanne GERVILLE-RÉACHE (ms)
La Vivandière : Viens avec nous (Godard)
(B 8333-3) 5- 5-11 V. 87080
Werther : Va! laisse-les couler (Massenet)
(B 7022-2) 29- 4-09 V. 81097 *IRCC 109*
AGSA 2 Enrico CARUSO (t)
Sei morta ne la vita mia (Costa)
(B 21774-2) 16- 4-18 (V. 87293)
Noche feliz - Canción mexicana (Posadas)
(B 24460-4) 14- 9-20 (V. 87366) d.s.V. 958
AGSA 3 Giovanni ZENATELLO (t)
Manon Lescaut : Ah ! Manon, mi tradisce (Puccini)
(BVE 49818-2) 31- 1-29 V. 1399
Giovanni ZENATELLO (t) Maria GAY (c)
Tosca : Tu ? di tua man ... O dolci mani (Puccini)
(BVE 49808-1) 29- 1-29 V. 1399
AGSA 4 Lillian BLAUVELT (s)
Les Vêpres Siciliennes : Bolero (Merci, Compagnons) (Verdi)
(B 421 2) 13- 4-05 V. 81067 *IRCC 8*
Pauline DONALDA (s)
Faust : Air des bijoux (Gounod)
(8453 b) 9- 7-06 G. 33620 *IRCC 46*
AGSA 5 Edmond CLÉMENT (t) Geraldine FARRAR (s)
Danté : Nous allons partir (Godard)
(C 12910-2) 17- 3-13 V. 87508
Sous la fenêtre (Unter'm Fenster) (Schumann op.34 No.3)
(B 12911-4) 17- 3-13 V. 86507
AGSA 6 NOT USED
AGSA 7 Charles DALMORÈS (t)
Les Contes d'Hoffmann : C'est elle (Offenbach)
(B 6046-3) 25- 3-08 V. 87089
Les Contes d'Hoffmann : Ô Dieux, de quelle ivresse (Offenbach)
(B 6048-1) 1908 V. Unp. 1st. Issue
AGSA 8 Frances ALDA (s)
Manon Lescaut : In quelle trine morbide (Puccini)

(B 45658-3) 26- 6-28 V. 1474
Manon Lescaut : L'ora, o Tirsi (Puccini)
(B 10188-2) 6-3-28 V. 1474
AGSA 9 Frances ALDA (s)
La Cena delle Beffe : Sempre così (Giordano)
(BVE 32816-5) 20- 5-25 V. 1359
La Cena delle Beffe : Mi chiamano Lisabeta (Giordano)
(BVE 34361-2) 12- 2-26 V. 1359
AGSA 10 Titta RUFFO (b)
La Forza del Destino : Urna fatale del mio destino (Verdi)
(B 15892-1) 14- 4-15 V. Unp. *HRS 2015*
Nabucco : Che tenti ? ... Tremin gl'insani (Verdi)
(B 14518) 26- 2-14 V. 87194
AGSA 11 Feodor Ivanovich CHALIAPIN (bs)
La Bohème : Vecchia zimarra (Puccini)
(B 29247-2) 3- 1-24 V. Unp. 1st. Issue
Antonina NEZHDANOVA (s)
Mtisri : The Song of the fish (Arensky)
(7220 L) 1908 G. 2-33318
AGSA 12 NOT USED
AGSA 13 Carlo ALBANI (t)
Andrea Chénier : Come un bel dì di maggio (Giordano)
(B 4890-1) 22-10-07 V. Unp. 1st. Issue
Tosca : Recondita armonia (Puccini)
(B 4897-1) 28-10-07 V. Unp. 1st. Issue
AGSA 14 Frances ALDA (s)
La Bohème : Donde lieta usci (Puccini)
(B 14497-1) 20- 2-14 V. Unp. (64417)
1st. Issue
Gianni Schicchi : O mio babbino caro (Puccini)
(B 22758-2) 11- 2-19 V. 68402
AGSA 15 Charles DALMORÈS (t)
Le Prophète : Roi, du ciel (Meyerbeer)
(B 4395-3) 25- 3-08 V. Unp. *IRCC 131*
Samson e Dalila : Arrêtez, ô mes frères ! (Saint-Saëns)
(B 11153-2) V. 87087
AGSA 16 Titta RUFFO (b)
Hamlet : Spettro santo (Thomas)
(10897 b) 1907 G. 2-52621
Hamlet : Spettro infernale (Spectre infernal) (Thomas)
(10898½ b) 1907 G. 2-52622
AGSA 17 Charles GILIBERT (b) Gabrielle LEJEUNE (ms)
Maria DUCHÊNE (c) Suzanne DUMESNIL (s)

David DEVRIES (t) F. LEROUX (t)
Carmen : Non métier est bon (Bizet)
(B 8745-1) not known V. Unp. 1st. Issue
Maria GAY (c)
Carmen : Presso il bastion di Siviglia (Près des ramparts Séville) (Bizet)
(7293 e) -12-07 G. 53516

AGSA 18 Selma KURZ (s)
Ave Maria (G) (Tosti)
(9890 u) 1906 G. 43898
Manon : Nützet die schönen jungen Tage
(Obéissons quand leur) (Massenet)
(15029 b) 26-10-10G. 2-43381

AGSA 19 NOT USED

AGSA 20 Titta RUFFO (b)
Malena : Mi sfiorita (Titta)
(10548 b) 1907 G. 2-52623
Malena : Disse il saggio (Titta)
(10549 b) 1907 G. 2-52624

AGSA 21 John McCORMACK (t)
The Bitterness of love (Dunn)
(Bb 21040-2) 4-12-30 G. DA.1175
Three aspects (Parry)
(Bb 21029-2) 3-12-30 G. DA.1172

AGSA 22 Antonio PAOLI (t)
Déjanire : Epitalame (It) (*Viens ô toi*) (Saint-Saëns)
(1180 ah) 30- 6-11 G. 2-52808
Samson e Dalila : Figli miei (*Arrêtez, ô mes frères !*) (Saint-Saëns)
(10521 b) 1907 G. 2-52597

AGSA 23 Giovanni MARTINELLI (t)
Zazà : È un riso gentil (Leoncavallo)
(A 26164-4) 15-11-27 V. Unp. 1st. Issue
Apollo GRANFORTE (b)
Zazà : Zazà, piccola zingara (Leoncavallo)
(BM 1188-1) 29-10-29 G. 7-52433

AGSA 24 Mattia BATTISTINI (b)
Don Giovanni : Finch' han dal vino (Mozart)
(439 z) 1902 G. 52663 *HRS 1007*
Il Barbiere di Siviglia : Largo al factotum (Rossini)
(447 z) 1902 G. 52671 *IRCC 77*

AGSA 25 Fernando DE LUCIA (t) Ernesto BADINI (b)
L'Elisir d'Amore : Obbligato (Donizetti)
(10513 b) 1907 G. 54357
Fernando DE LUCIA (t)

Manon : Chiudo gli occhi (La rêve : En ferment les yeux) (Massenet)
(10515 b) 1907 G. 2-52607 *IRCC 57*

AGSA 26 NOT USED

AGSA 27 Enrico CARUSO (t)
Amadis de Gaul : Bois épais (Lully)
(B 24465-6) 16- 9-20 V. d.s. 1437

(AGSA 27 rr) Enrico CARUSO (t)
Première Caresse (de Crescenzo)
(B 23144-4) 9- 9-19 V. d.s. 1437 rr

AGSA 28 Giacomo LAURI VOLPI (t)
La Gioconda : Assassini ! (Ponchielli)
(B 51148-2) 10- 4-29 V. 3052
Les Contes d'Hoffmann : Légende de Kleinzach (Offenbach)
(B 51149-2) 10- 4-29 V. 3052

AGSA 29 Dinh GILLY (b)
La Coupe du Roi de Thulé: Il est venu ce jour de lutte (1) (Diaz)
(Bb 3357-2) 24- 8-23 G. 7-32082
La Coupe du Roi de Thulé: Il aurait vu son amour (2) (Diaz)
(Bb 3358-1) 24- 8-23 G. 7-32083

AGSA 30 Mattia BATTISTINI (b)
Un Ballo in Maschera : Alla vita che t'arride (Verdi)
(BK 1422-1) 22- 2-24 G. 7-52264
Don Giovanni : Deh, vieni alla finestra (Mozart)
(BK 1433-3) 27- 2-24 G. 7-52265

AGSA 31 Mattia BATTISTINI (b)
La Favorite : Vien Leonora (Léonore ! viens) (Donizetti)
(17570 b) 2- 6-13 G. 2-52848
La Favorite : Dei nemici tuoi (Léonore! mon amour brave) (Donizetti)
(17571 b) 2- 6-13 G. 2-52849

AGSA 32 Pol PLANÇON (bs)
Le Châlet : Vallons de l'Helvétia (Adam)
(B 1050-1) 27- 2-04 V. 81037 *IRCC 25*
Roméo et Juliette : Allons ! Jeunes gens (Gounod)
(B 990-1) 29- 1-04 V. 81035

AGSA 33 Zelie DE LUSSAN (s)
Lili (Lola mine) (Guétary)
(A 2187 - B 16-1) 17- 5-03 V. 2187 *IRCC 69*
La Paloma (Yradier)
(A 2301 - B17-1) 17- 5-03 V. 2301

AGSA 34 Kirsten FLAGSTAD (s)
Lykken mellem to Mennesker (Alnaes)
(BN 191-2) 19- 1-29 G. 7-283352
Saeterjentens Sondag (Bull)

(BN 192-2) 19- 1-29G. 7-283354

AGSA 35 Kirsten FLAGSTAD (s)

Sne (Rode)

(BN 190-1) 19- 1-29 G. 7-283351

Peer Gynt : Solvejs Sang (Grieg)

(BN 193-1) 19- 1-29 G. 7-283353

AGSA 36 Johanna GADSKI (s)

Götterdämmerung : Betrug ! Schändlichster Betrug ! (Wagner)

(B 8924-2) 7- 5-10 V. Unp. *IRCC 128*

Götterdämmerung : Helle Wehr ! (Wagner)

(B 8608-1) 7- 2-10 V. 87052

AGSA 37 - 44 NOT USED

AGSA 45 Pol PLANÇON (bs)

La Damnation de Faust : Sérénade (Devant la maison) (Berlioz)

(B 3024-1) 23- 1-06 V. 81034

Martha : Chi mi dirà (Porterlied) (Flotow)

(A 4346-1) 27- 3-07 V. 81086 *IRCC 133*

AGSA 46 John McCORMACK (t)

Holy God, we praise Thy name ! (arr. Walworth)

(B 29870-2) 9- 4-24 V. Unp. 1st. Issue

I saw from the beach (arr. Hughes)

(Bb 5519-1) 24- 9-24 G. 6-2041

AGSA 47 John McCORMACK (t)

The Singers consolation (Sangers trost) (Schumman op.127 No.1)

(B 23799-2) 2- 4-20 V. Unp. 1st. Issue

Die liebe hat gelogen (Schubert)

(B 28610) 26- 9-23 V. Unp. 1st. Issue

AGSA 48 John McCORMACK (t)

Die Mainacht (Brahms op.43 No.2)

(Bb 5031-2) 4- 9-24 G. 7-42085

In Waldheimsamkeit (Schubert op.85 No.6)

(Bb 5032-2) 4- 9-24 G. 7-42086

AGSA 49 John McCORMACK (t)

Luoghi sereni e cari (Donaudy)

(Bb 5033-2) 4- 9-24 G. 7-52275

O del mio amato ben (Donaudy)

(Bb 5035-1) 4- 9-24 G. 7-52276 *IRCC 217*

AGSA 50 John McCORMACK (t)

Komm' bald (Brahms op.97 No.5)

(Bb 5094-2) 19- 9-24 G. 7-42087 *IRCC 62*

Feldeinsamkeit (Brahms op.86 No.2)

(Bb 5095-1) 19- 9-24 G. 7-42088 *IRCC 62*

AGSA 51 John McCORMACK (t)

Dream on, little soldier (I. Berlin)
(B 22253-1) 24- 9-18 V. Unp. 1st. Issue
Sometime (I'll hear your sweet voice) (Lockwood)
(B 28607-2) 27- 9-23 V. 1003

AGSA 52 John McCORMACK (t)
The lass with the delicate air (Arne arr.Lehman)
(0EA 8822-1) 11- 7-40 G. Unp. 1st. Issue
The little boats (Boulton arr.Hughes)
(0EA 9328-1) 25- 6-41 G. (IR 1057).1st. Issue

AGSA 53 John McCORMACK (t)
Love thee, dearest, love thee (Moore - old air)
(0EA 9869-1) 26- 5-42 G. Unp. 1st. Issue
IR 1053 (Iss.1956)
The green bushes (trad. arr.Keel)
(0EA 9358-1) 26- 8-4 1 G. Unp. 1st. Issue

AGSA 54 John McCORMACK (t)
Maureen - Irish cradle song (Roberton)
(0EA 9461-1) 26- 8-41 G. Unp. 1st. Issue
Off to Philadelphia (Haynes)
(0EA 9655-1) 3-12-41 G. Unp. 1st. Issue
IR 1056 (iss.1956)

AGSA 55 John McCORMACK (t)
The gentle maiden (trad arr.Somervel)
(0EA 8851-1) 9- 8-40 G. (DA.1760) IR 1043
Dawn will break (Haydn Wood)
(0EA 9314-1) 29- 5-41 G. Unp. 1st. Issue

AGSA 56 John McCORMACK (t)
Oft in the stilly night (Trad arr.Schneider)
(0EA 8849-1) 9-8-40 G. (DA.1760) IR 1043
Robin Hood : Oh promise me (de Koven)
(0EA 9487-1) 6-10-41 G. (IR 1053) 1st. Issue

AGSA 57 John McCORMACK (t)
Charm me to sleep (asleep) (Herrick Sanderson)
(0B 3855-1) 16- 9-32 G. DA.1287
Passing by (Edward Purcell)
(0EA 8824-1) 11- 7-40 G. Unp. 1st. Issue

AGSA 58 John McCORMACK (t)
When I awake (Wright)
(0EA 9084-1) 28- 1-41 G. (IR 1046) 1st. Issue
Waiting for you (Phillips)
(0EA 9278-1) 10- 9-42 G. (IR 1046) 1st. Issue

AGSA 59 John McCORMACK (t)
The village that nobody knows (Haydn Wood)

		(0EA 9315-1)	7- 9-33	G. Unp. 1st. Issue
	The blind ploughman (Clarke)			
		(0EA 9063-1)	17-12-40	G. Unp. 1st. Issue
AGSA	60	John McCORMACK (t)		
	At the mid hour of night (Trad arr.Stanford)			
		(0EA 9083-1)	28- 1-41	G. IR 1044
	By the lakes of Killarney (Case)			
		(0EA 9868-1)	26- 5-42	G. IR 1044
AGSA	61	John McCORMACK (t)		
	Nina (Tre giorni son che Nina) (Ciampi)			
		(0EA 8807-1)	19- 6-40	G. Unp. 1st. Issue
	To Chloë (Mozart K.524)			
		(0EA 9277-1)	10- 9-42	G. (IR 1045) 1st. Issue
AGSA	62	John McCORMACK (t)		
	Under the spell of the rose (Easthope Martin)			
		(BVE 49240)	7-12-28	V. Unp. 1st. Issue
	Song o' my heart (Hanley)			
		(B 58690-1)	10- 3-30	V. Unp. 1st. Issue
AGSA	63	John McCORMACK (t)		
	When you're in love (Blaufuss)			
		(B 38731-5)	11-10-27	V. Unp. 1st. Issue
	Fallen leaf - Indian love song (Logan)			
		(BVE 38387- 5)	4- 5-27	V. Unp. 1st. Issue
AGSB	1	Ernestine SCHUMANN-HEINK (c)		
	Das Rheingold : Weiche, Wotan, weiche (Wagner)			
		(C 55615-2)	17- 7-29	V. 7107
	Götterdämmerung :Höre mit Sinn (Wagner)			
		(C 55616-1)	17- 7-29	V. 7107
AGSB	2	Lauritz MELCHIOR (t)		
	L'Africaine : Land so wunderbar (Pays merveilleux) (Meyerbeer)			
		(Cc 19612-1)	29- 5-30	G. EJ 582
	I Pagliacci : Jetz spielen (Recitar ... Vesti la giubba) (Leoncavallo)			
		(Cc 19608-1)	29- 5-30	G. EJ 582
AGSB	3	John McCORMACK (t)		
	Natoma : Paul's address (No Country can my own outvie) (Herbert)			
		(C 11822-1)	3- 4-12	V. 74295
	La Traviata : Lunge da lei ... De' miei bollenti spiriti (Verdi)			
		(C 8693-1)	10- 3-10	V. Unp. G. 2-052025 *IRCC 96*
AGSB	4	Mattia BATTISTINI (b)		
	L'Africaine : Quando amor m'accende (Meyerbeer)			
		(215 af)	25- 5-12	G. 052358

L'Africaine : Averla tanto amata (Avoir tant adorée) (Meyerbeer)
(216 af) 25- 5-12 G. 052359

AGSB 5 Emma EAMES (s)
Les Chanson des Baisers (Bemberg)
(C 6206-1) 19- 5-08 V. 88133 *IRCC 90*
Dopo (Tosti)
(C 11307-1) 27-11-11 V. 88344 *IRCC 43*

AGSB 6 Emma CALVÉ (s)
Cavalleria Rusticana : Voi lo sapete o mamma (Mascagni)
(C 4426-1) 22- 4-07 V. 88086
La Perle du Brésil : Charmant oiseau (David)
(C 6024-1) 9- 3-08 V. 88087

AGSB 7 Dame Nellie MELBA (s)
Hamlet : A vos jeux, mes amis (Pâle et Blonde) (Thomas)
(C 4354-1) 29- 3-07 V. 88069
Hamlet : Et maintenant écoutez (Thomas)
(C 4355-1) 29- 3-07 V. 88070

AGSB 8 Feodor Ivanovich CHALIAPIN (bs)
Demon : Do not weep my child (Rubinstein)
(2495c) 15-10-11 G. 022225
Feodor Ivanovich CHALIAPIN (bs) Maria KOVALENKO (s)
Demon : On the airy ocean (Rubinstein)
(2536c) 12-11-11 G. 022262

AGSB 9 Charles DALMORÈS (t)
Il Trovatore : Ah ! sì ben mio coll'essere (Verdi)
(C 4394-1) 12- 4-07 V. 85123 *HRS 1001*
Grisélidis :Ouvrez-vous sur mon front (Massenet)
(C 12538-1) 25-10-12 V. 88397

AGSB 10 Lotte SCHÖNE (s) Willi DOMGRAF-FASSBAENDER (b)
Don Paquale : Pronto io son (Donizetti)
(2D 270-1) 24- 3-31 G. DB.1546
Don Pasquale : Vado, corro (Donizetti)
(2D 271-1) 24- 3-31 G. DB.1546

AGSB 11 NOT USED

AGSB 12 Johanna GADSKI (s) Albert REISS (t)
The Bartered Bride : Ich weiss Euch einen lieben schatz (Smetana)
(C 7025-1) 30- 4-09 V. Unp *IRCC 140*
Emmy DESTINN (s)
Dalibor : Wär'es wahr ? (Smetana)
(273 ac) 18-10-09 G. 043138
IRCC 184

AGSB 13 Dinh GILLY (b)
Le Jongleur de Notre Dame : La Viérge entend fort bien (1) (Massenet)

(Cc 3355-1)   24- 8-24   G. 2-032076

Le Jongleur de Notre Dame : Fleurissait un rose (2) (Massenet)

(Cc 3356-2)   24- 8-24   G. 2-032077

AGSB 14   Claudia MUZIO (s)

La Bohème : Sì, mi chiamano Mimì (Puccini)

(298 aj)   20- 6-11   G. 053264 *IRCC 39*

Blanche ARRAL (s)

Les Noces de Jeannette : Chant du rossignol (Massé)

(C 6911-1)   V. 74142

AGSB 15   Emma EAMES (s) Emilio DE GOGORZA (b)

Die Zauberflöte : Là dove prende (Bei Männern) (Mozart)

(C 3171-3)   9- 3-06   V. 89003

Il Trovatore : Mira d'acerbe lagrime (Verdi)

(C 6233-5)   6- 4 -09   V. 89022 *IRCC 113*

AGSB 16   Frances ALDA (s)

Falstaff : Sul fil d'un soffio (Verdi)

(C 8883-1)   25- 4-10   V. 88213 *IRCC 111*

Il Segreto di Susanna : O gioia, la nube (Wolf-Ferrari)

(C 14495-1)   20- 2-14   V. 74338

AGSB 17   Ernestine SCHUMANN-HEINK (c)

Le Prophète : Scène de la prison (1) *(O Prêtres de Baal)* (Meyerbeer)

(C 4838-2)   26- 9-07   V. 88094 *IRCC 93 ?*

Le Prophète : Prison aria (2) *(Il va venir)* (Meyerbeer)

(C 4839-1)   26- 9-07   V. 88095 *IRCC 93 ?*

AGSB 18   Enrico CARUSO (t)

Eugene Onegin : Pour moi ce jour (Lensky's aria Act 3) (Tchaikovsky)

(C 18657 1)   3-11-16   V. 88582

(AGSB 18 rr)   Enrico CARUSO (t)

L'Africaine : Che dicon mai ...Deh ! ch'io ritorni (Meyerbeer)

(C 24464-5)   16- 9-20   V. d.s. 7156 rr

AGSB 19   Charles DALMORÈS (t) Marcel JOURNET (bs)

Carmen : Je suis Escamillo (Bizet)

(C 4253-1)   19- 2-07   V. 85115 *IRCC 169*

Faust : Ô merveille (Gounod)

(C 4254-2)   19- 2-07   V. 85115 *IRCC 169*

AGSB 20   Giovanni ZENATELLO (t) w.Ch.

Un Ballo in Maschera : Su profetessa ... Di' tu se fedele (Verdi)

(C 59365-1)   3- 3-30   V. 7236

Giovanni ZENATELLO (t) Gloria MARION A. BOEMI Ch.

Un Ballo in Maschera : Ella e pura ... Ah ! morte infamia (Verdi)

(C 59366-4)   12- 3-30   V. 7236

AGSB 21   Ernestine SCHUMANN-HEINK (c)

La Clemenza di Tito : Parto, parto (Mozart)

(C 8231-3) 18- 9-09 V. 88196
Louise Kirkby LUNN
La Clemenza di Tito : Non più di fiori (Mozart)
(z 5500 f) 22- 9-11 G. 2-053068
IRCC 147

AGSB 22 Emma EAMES (s)
Spring (Henschel) *
Year's at the Spring (Beach)
(C 6203-1) 18- 5-08 V. 88008
IRCC 194

* Note: In his authorative article on Eames (*The Record Collector* Vol.8 No.4), Louis Migliori gives the impression that this record was made before, and with the same matrix number as the *L'incredule / Year's at the Spring coupling*. This was a mistaken assumption. (See IRCC 125 & IRCC 194)

Gretchen am Spinnrade (Schubert)
(C 11312-2) 28-11-11 V. 88367
IRCC 76

AGSB 23 Johanna GADSKI (s)
Lobentanz : An allen Zweigen (Thiulle)
(C 11528-4) 14-3-12 V. 88362
Die Wacht am Rhein (Wilhelm)
(C 15690-2) 8- 2-15 V. 88515

AGSB 24 Antonio SCOTTI (b)
Rigoletto : Deh, non parlare al misero (Verdi)
Don Giovanni : Finch'han dal vino (Mozart)
(C 1094-1) 10- 3-04 V. 85031 *IRCC 18*
L'Elisir d'Amore : Come Paride vezzoso (Donizetti)
(C 2361-1) 2- 3-05 V. 85068 *IRCC 90*

AGSB 25 Geraldine FARRAR (s) Edmond CLÉMENT (t)
Roméo et Juliette : Ange adorable (Gounod)
(C 12912-1) 13- 2-13 V. 88421
Mefistofele : In me fuggi lo sguardo ! ... Lontano, lontano (Boïto)
(C 12913-2) 13- 2-13 V. 88422

AGSB 26 Frida LEIDER (s)
Don Giovanni : Or sai che l'onore (Mozart)
(CR 2010-1) 11- 5-28 G. 2-053325
Armide : Ah ! sì la liberté (Gluck)
(CR 2012-2A) 11- 5-28 G. 2-033133

AGSB 27 Jose MARDONES (bs)
Nabucco : Tu sul labbro de'veggenti (Verdi)
(C 27332) 6- 2-23 V. 74854
Les Vêpres Siciliennes : O tu Palermo (Et toi Palerme) (Verdi)
(C 27331-1) 19-12-22 V. 74808

AGSB 28 Titta RUFFO (b)
Cristoforo Colombo : Aman lassù le stelle (Franchetti)
(C 14517) 26- 2-14 V. 88486
Cristoforo Colombo : Dunque ho sognato (Franchetti)
(C 25213) 14- 4-21 V. 88668

AGSB 29 Frieda HEMPEL (s)
Mireille : O d'amor messagera (Ô légère hirondelle) (Gounod)
(609 m) 9- 4-12 G. 053290
Robert le Diable : Robert, toi que j'aime (Meyerbeer)
(720 m) 30- 5-13 G. 033165

AGSB 30 - 35 NOT USED

AGSB 36 Johanna GADSKI (s)
Götterdämmerung : Fliegt heim (Wagner)
(C 7030-1) 1 - 5-09 V. 88185
Götterdämmerung : Zu neuen Thaten (Wagner)
(C 8599-1) 7- 2-10 V. Unp. 1st. Issue

AGSB 37 - 42 NOT USED

AGSB 44 Mary GARDEN (s)
Louise : Depuis le jour (Maeterlinck)
(CVE 36734-14) 24-12-26 V. 6623
Resurrection : Voici l'heure ... Dieu de grâce (Alfano)
(CVE 36735-6) 3-11-26 V. 6623

AGSB 45 Maria NEMETH (s) Emil SCHIPPER (b)
Aïda : Wehe ! mein Vater (Ciel mio padre) (Verdi)
(CW 2504-1) 3- 5-29 G. 2-044068
Aïda : Wohlan denn, erhebt Euch (Su, dunque) (Verdi)
(CW 2505-2) 3- 5 29 G. EJ 491

AGSB 46 Emma CALVÉ (s)
Ma Lisette (trad. arr. Massenet)
Au printemps (Gounod)
(C 6018-1) 6- 3-08 V. 88123
Chanson espagnole (Yradier)
(C 6023-1) V. 63003

AGSB 47 Selma KURZ (s)
I Puritani : Qui la voce (Bellini)
(573 m) 28- 9-11 G. 053277
I Puritani : Vien diletto (Bellini)
(574 m) 28- 9-11 G. 053278

AGSB 48 Emmy DESTINN (s)
Der Freischütz : Wie nahte nir der Schlummer (Weber)
(206 z) 29-10-10 G. 043158
Der Freischütz : Und ob die Wolke (Weber)
(207 z) 29-10-10 G. 043163

AGSB 49 Beniamino GIGLI (t) Titta RUFFO (b)
La Forza del Destino : Solenne in quest'ora (Verdi)
(C 37319-2) 17-12-26 V. Unp. 1st. Issue
La Gioconda : Enzo Grimaldo, Principe di Santafior (Ponchielli)
(C 37321-1) 17-12-26 V. Unp. 1st. Issue

AGSB 50 Enrico CARUSO (t) Geraldine FARRAR (s)
La Bohème : O soave fanciulla (Puccini)
(C 12751-1) 30-12-12 V. Unp. *IRCC 61*
Geraldine FARRAR (s) Josephine JACOBY (c)
Madama Butterfly : Tutti i fior (Puccini)
(C 8268-2) 2-10-09 V. 89026

AGSB 51 Geraldine FARRAR (s) Giovanni MARTINELLI (t)
Carmen : Halte-là ! qui va là ! (Bizet)
(C 16030-2) 17- 5-15 V. 88536
Carmen : Au quartier pour l'appel (Bizet)
(C 16031-4) 19- 5-15 V. Unp. (88532) *IRCC 58*

AGSB 52 Mattia BATTISTINI (b)
Per la Patria : Or limpida Bella (Cocchi)
(866 c) 12-11-06 G. 052140
Zampa : Perchè tremar ? (Hérold)
(889 c) -11-06 G. 052148 *IRCC 202*

AGSB 53 Dame Nellie MELBA (s)
The white sea mist (Ronald)
(C 6699-2) 1- 1-09 V. Unp (G. 03134) *IRCC* 52
Anges pleurent (Bemberg)
Chant Vénetian (Bemberg)
(C 13908-1) 4-10-13 V. Unp. (88057) 1st. Issue

AGSB 54 Pasquale AMATO (b)
Dinorah : Sei vendicata assai (Ah ! Mon remords te venge) (Meyerbeer)
(C 14534-2) 4- 3-14 V. 88473
Tosca : Tre sbirri ... Te Deum (Puccini)
(C 14715-2) 16- 4-14 V. 88489

AGSB 55 Geraldine FARRAR (s)
Tosca : Ora stammi a sentir (Puccini)
(C 9834-2) 26- 1-11 V. 88287
Roméo et Juliette : Valse (Je veux vivre) (Gounod)
(C 9855-1) 26- 1-11 V. Unp. *IRCC 114*

AGSB 56 Beniamino GIGLI (t)
Les Pêcheurs de Perles : Mi par d'udire ancora (Je crois entendre encore) (Bizet)
(CVE 58119-3) 18-12-29 V. Unp. 1st. Issue
Beniamino GIGLI (t) & Titta RUFFO (b)

La Bohème : In un coupé ... O Mimì, tu più non torni (Puccini)
(C 37320-2) 17-12-26 V. Unp. 1st. Issue

AGSB 57 Giacomo LAURI VOLPI (t)
Les Huguenots : Bianca al par (Plus blanche) (Meyerbeer)
(C 41449-2 (?)) 16- 1-28 V. Unp. 1st. Issue
Faust : Salut ! Demure chaste et pure (Gounod)
(C 58627-1) 29- 1-30 V. 7389

AGSB 58 Beniamino GIGLI (t) Lucrezia BORI (s)
Roméo et Juliette : Ange adorable (Gounod)
(C 27714-1) 28- 3-23 V. Unp.1st. Issue
Miguel FLETA (t) Lucrezia BORI (s)
Carmen : Parle-moi de ma mère (Bizet)
(C 29286-2) 14- 1-24 V. Unp. *HRS 1039*

AGSB 59 Frieda HEMPEL (s)
Der Wildschütz : Auf des lebens raschen Wogen (Lortzing)
(1174 s) 18-9-13 G. 043247 *IRCC 161*
Les Huguenots : Ô beau pays de la Tourraine (Meyerbeer)
(2222 c) 9- 6-11 G. 033125

AGSB 60 Emma EAMES (s)
Carmen : Air de Micaëla (Jes dis que rien ne m'épouvante) (Bizet)
(C 3386-1) 14- 5-06 V. 88036 *IRCC 32*
Si tu le veux (Massenet)
Cherubin : Aubade (Massenet)
(C 6202-1) 18- 5-08 V. 88135 *IRCC 76*

AGSB 61 Rita FORNIA (s)
Faust : Le parlate d'amor (Faites-lui mes aveux) (Gounod)
(C 8659 2) 25- 2-10 V. Unp. 1st. Issue
Roméo et Juliette : Chanson de Stephano (Gounod)
(C 9738-1) 23-12-10 V. 74211

AGSB 62 NOT USED

AGSB 63 Edward JOHNSON (t)
La Fanciulla del West : Una parola sola ... Or son sei mesi (Puccini)
(C 23460) 7-11-19 V. Unp. 1st. Issue
Bernardo DE MURO (t)
La Fanciulla del West : Sono Ramerrez (Puccini)
(1056-2 aj) 17- 5-20 G. 2-052176

AGSB 64 Mario ANCONA (b)
Ernani : O de' verd'anni miei (Verdi)
(C 4284-1) 6- 3-07 V. 88062
Faust : Non val, perchè mai (Ecoute-moi bien) (Gounod)
(C 4992-1) 6- 1-08 V. (88109)
IRCC 130

AGSB 65 Carlo ALBANI (t)

Andrea Chénier : Un dì all'azzurro spazio (Improvviso) (Giordano)
(C 4898-1) 28-10-07 V. Unp. *HRS 1053*
Lucrezia Borgia : Di pescator ignobile (Donizetti)
(C 4887-1) 18-10-07 V. 74098 *HRS 1003*

AGSB 66 Helen Beach YAW (s)
La Perle du Brésil : Charmant oiseseau (David)
(C 4827-2) 24- 9-07 V. Unp. 1st. Issue
Lucia di Lammermoor : Ardon gl'incensi (Donizetti)
(C 4834-1) 25- 9-07 V. Unp. *HRS 1026*

AGSB 67 Dame Nellie MELBA (s)
Down in the forest (Ronald)
(C 6698-1) 1- 1-09 V. Unp. *IRCC 52*
O lovely night (Ronald)
(C 6706-2) 6- 1-09 V. 88182

AGSB 68 NOT USED

AGSB 69 Emilio DE GOGORZA (b)
Le Mariage (Widor)
Le Planquier (Widor)
(C 6200-1) 1908 V. Unp. ?
Benvenuto Cellini : De l'art splendour immortelle (Diaz)
(C 6765-1) V. Unp. 1st. Issue

AGSB 70 Mabel GARRISON (s)
Les Huguenots : Nobil signori salute
(Nobles Seigneurs, salut!) (Meyerbeer)
(C 27798)
L'Eclair : Call me thine own (Halévy)
(C 23742) V. 74612

AGSB 71 Antonina NEZHDANOVA (s)
The Demon : The night was warm (R) (Rubinstein)
(398 ac) 9- 5-11 G. 023075
Der Vogel im Walde (R) (Taubert)
(1927c) 27- 1-10 G. 023047

AGSB 72 Dmitri Alexeyevich SMIRNOV (t) Maria DAVIDOV (ms)
Boris Godunov : Oh Tsarevitch, I implore thee (R) (Mussorgsky)
(Cc 3335-1) 21- 8-23 G. 2-024000
Dmitri Alexeyevich SMIRNOV (t)
The Fair at Sorotchinski : Pourquoi mon triste coeur (Mussorgsky)
(Cc 4720-1) 12- 6-24 G. 2-032081

AGSB 73 Charles GILIBERT (b) Gabrielle LEJEUNE (s) F. LEROUX (t)
Maria DUCHÊNE (c) Suzanne DUMESNIL (ms)
Carmen : Quintet (Nous avons en tête) (Bizet)
(C 8746-1) 1910 V. 88237
Charles GILIBERT (b)

La Jolie Fille de Perth : Quand la flamme (Bizet)
(C 8489-2) 28- 1-10 V. 72408

AGSB 74 Pol PLANÇON (bs)
Mignon : Del suo cor calmai le pene (Berceuse) (Thomas)
(C 6112-1) 14- 4-08 V. 85126 *IRCC 94*
Stabat Mater : Pro peccatis (Rossini)
(C 6113-1) 14- 4-08 V. Unp. *IRCC 81*

AGSB 75 Clara BUTT (c)
Lucrezia Borgia : Brindisi (Il segreto per essere felice) (Donizetti)
(3487 f) 16- 7-09 G. 2-033010
Sosarme : Rend' il sereno al ciglio (Handel)
(Ac 6382 f) 24- 7-12 G. 2-053088

AGSB 76 - 78 NOT USED

AGSB 79 (Augustin) Francisco NUIBO (t)
Faust : Salut ! demeure chaste et pure (Gounod)
(C 2205-1) 25- 1-05 V. Unp. 1st. Issue
Mireille : Mon coeur ... Ange du paradis (Gounod)
(C 2222-1) 7- 2-05 V. Unp. 1st. Issue

AGSB 80 Amelita GALLI-CURCI (s)
Il Trovatore : Tacea la notte placida ... Di tale amor (Verdi)
(C 28469-3) 13- 9-23 V. Unp. G. 2-053233
Il Trovatore : D'amor sull'ali rosee (Verdi)
(C 30297-8) 16- 9-24 V. Unp. G. 2-053234

AGSB 81 Ernestine SCHUMANN-HEINK (c)
Rienzi : Gerechter Gott (Wagner)
(C 6478-1) 29- 9-08 V. 88140
Hermann JADLOWKER (t)
Rienzi : Allmächter'ger Vater (Wagner)
(1339 s) 10- 2-14 G. 042457

AGSB 82 Fernand ANSSEAU (t)
Joseph : Champs paternels (Méhul)
(HO 4447-2 af) 29- 6-20 G. 2-032057
La Damnation de Faust : Nature immense (Berlioz)
(CS 832-2) 26- 2-23 G. 2-032072

AGSB 83 Eidé NORÉNA (s)
Hamlet : Sa main depuis hier (1) (Thomas)
(2PG 908-1) 27- 6-33 G. 52-1206 DB.4902
Hamlet : Il garde la silence (2) (Thomas)
(2PG 909-1) 27- 6-33 G. 52-1207 DB.4902

AGSA 84NOT USED

AGSB 85 Jean- Émile VANNI-MARCOUX (bs)
Don Carlos : Elle ne m'aimes pas (Verdi)
(2W 612-2) 7-10-31 DB. 4823

Don Carlos : Je dormirai dans mon manteau royal (Verdi)
(2W 613-2) 7-10-31 DB. 4823

AGSB 86 Leonid Vitalyevich SOBINOV (t)
Eugene Onegin : Whither have you gone ? (R) (Tchaikovsky)
(1986c) 6- 2-10 G. 022140
Eugene Onegin : I love you Olga (R) (Tchaikovsky)
(2516 c) 31-10-11 G. 022243

AGSB 87 Marcella SEMBRICH (s)
Halka : Gdyby rannem slonkiem (Polish) (Moniuszko)
(C 4860-2) 5-10-07 V. 88101 *IRCC 129*
Zyczenie (The Maiden's Wish) (Polish) (Chopin)
(C 4875-1) 9-10-07 V. 88100

AGSB 88 Marcella SEMBRICH (s)
Love me - Mazurka (Aime-moi) (Polish) (Chopin arr. Viardot)
(C 4874-1) 9-10-07 V. 88099
Si me vers avaient des ailes ! (Hahn)
Die Schöne Müllerin : Wohin ? (Schubert)
(C 5046-1) 30- 1-08 V. Unp. *IRCC 129*

AGSB 89 NOT USED

AGSB 90 Louise HOMER (ms)
Martha : Esser mesto il mio cuor (Flotow)
(C 3876-1) 12-10-06 V. 85105
Louise HOMER (ms) & Bessie ABOTT (s)
Martha : Mesta ognor (Flotow)
(C 4518-1) 21- 5-07 V. 89009

AGSB 91 Titta RUFFO (b)
La Favorite : Vien, Leonora (Léonore! viens) (Donizetti)
(z 6933 f) 24-12-12 G. 2-052075
Dinorah : Sei vendicata assai (Ah ! mon remords te venge) (Meyerbeer)
(C 14279-1) 8- 1-14 V. 88366

AGSB 92 Mario SAMMARCO (b)
Don Giovanni : Deh, vieni alla finestra (Mozart)
Falstaff : Quand'ero paggio (Verdi)
(3743 f) 21-10-09 G. 2-052013
Ernani : Lo vedremo (Verdi)
(5188 f) 15- 7-11 G. 2-052041

AGSB 93 Mattia BATTISTINI (b)
I Pagliacci : Sì può (Prologo) (1) (Leoncavallo)
(260 aj) 2- 6-11 G. 052305
I Pagliacci : Un nido di memorie (Prologo) (2) (Leoncavallo)
(261 aj) 2- 6-11 G. 052306

AGSB 94 Mattia BATTISTINI (b) Maria MOSCISCA (s)
I Pagliacci : Decidi il mio destin (Leoncavallo)

(221af) 28- 5-12 G. 054389
Mattia BATTISTINI (b) Maria MOSCISCA (s)
I Pagliacci : E allor perchè (Leoncavallo)
(222af) 28- 5-12 G. 054390

AGSB 95 - 201 NOT USED

AGSB 103 Ezio PINZA (bs)
Messa di Requiem: Confutatis maledictis (Verdi)
(CVE 51979-2) 7- 5-29 V. Unp. (8231)
1st. Issue
Il Trovatore : Abbietta zingara (Verdi)
(CVE 59746-1) 9- 4-30 V. Unp. (8231)
1st. Issue

AGSB 202 Helen Beach YAW (s)
Les Noces de Jeanette : Chant du rossignol (Massé)
(C 4830-2) 24- 9-07 V. 74092
Le Timbre d'Argent : Le bonheur est chose légère (Saint-Saëns)
(C 4835-2) 25- 9-07 V. Unp. *HRS 1026*

CONNOISSEURS RECORD CLUB (CRC)

According to *'Voices of the Past'* Vol. 6 pg. 185 these re-pressings were for : "International Record Collectors Club" (IRCC) - Blue Label records ABHB 1 and ABHB 2 "Connoisseurs Record Club" - Blue Label records ABHA 1, ABHB '3 to 7'

ABHA 1 Marcel JOURNET (bs)
La Régiment du Sambre et Meuse (Planquette)
(B 17059-1) 1- 1-16 V. Unp. 1st. Issue
Lucia di Lammermmor : Dalle stanze (Donizetti) (bs)
(B 17062-1) 1- 1-16 V. Unp.(66054)
1st. Issue

ABHB 1 Mattia BATTISTINI (b)
L'Africaine : Figlia che regi (Fille des Rois) (Meyerbeer)
(214 af) 25- 5-12 G. 052357
Il Guarany : Ola dunque ... Senza tetto (Gomez)
(CK 1432-3) 27- 2-24 G. 2-052257

ABHB 2 Mattia BATTISTINI (b)
Don Carlos : Felice ancor ... Per me giunto
(Il faut nous dire adieu ... C'est mon jour suprême) (Verdi)
(2808 c) 2- 6-13 G. 052404
Don Carlos : O Carlo ascolta ... Io morrò
(Carlos, écoute ... Ah je meurs) (Verdi)
(2809½ c) 2- 6-13 G. 052405

ABHB 3 Giovanni MARTINELLI (t) Rosa PONSELLE (s)
Aïda : La fatal pietra (Verdi)
(C 29451-2) 8- 2-24 V. Unp. 1st. Issue
Aïda : O terra addio (Verdi)
(C 29450-3) 8- 2-24 V. Unp. 1st. Issue

ABHB 4 Mattia BATTISTINI (b)
Macbeth : Perfidi ... Pietà, rispetto, amore (Verdi)
(234 af) 30- 5-12 G. 052369 *IRCC 202*
La Forza del Destino : Urna fatale (Verdi)
(CK 1418-1) 22- 2-24 G. 2-052251

ABHB 5 Selma KURZ (s)
Le Nozze di Figaro : Voi che sapete (Mozart)
(0750 v) 1907 G. 043110
Dinorah : Ombra leggiera (Ombre légère) (Meyerbeer)
(0821 v) 1908 G. 053179

ABHB 6 Fernando DE LUCIA (t) Josefina HUGUET (s)
La Traviata : Parigi o cara (Verdi)
(620 c) - 5-06 G. 054081
Rigoletto : È il sol dell'anima (Verdi)
(638 c) - 5-06 G. 054084

ABHB 7 Leonid Vitalyevich SOBINOV (t)
May Night : Sleep, my beauty (Rimsky-Korsakov)
(1988½ c) 6- 2-10 G. 022162
Snow Maiden : The joyous day departs (Rimsky-Korsakov)
(2216 c) 27- 2-11 G. 022199

DEUTSCHE GRAMMOFON

PM 78506e Francesco TAMAGNO (t)
ss. *Otello : Niun mi tema* (Verdi)
(269 I) - 4-04 G. 052068

P 80007 Enrico CARUSO (t)
Il Trovatore : Di quella pira (Verdi)
(B 3103-1) 11- 2-06 V. 87001 rr
G. 2-52489
Rigoletto : La donna è mobile (Verdi)
(B 6033-1) 16- 3-08 V. 87017

PM 85012 Enrico CARUSO (t)
La Bohème : Che gelida manina (Puccini)
(C 3101-1) 11-2-06 V. 88002
L'Elisir d'Amore : Una furtiva lagrima (Donizetti)
(C 996-2) 26-11-11 V. 88339

The first issue of re-pressings appeared in England in 1931. It was spearheaded by the then-very-young critic Desmond Shawe-Taylor and consisted of operatic titles by Lilli Lehmann . . .

In 1932, William Seltsam founded the International Record Collectors' Club (IRCC) and began a series of re-pressings that would run for about the next 20 years. Some of the earliest were from 10¾-inch masters and pressed by Columbia Records in the United States. . .

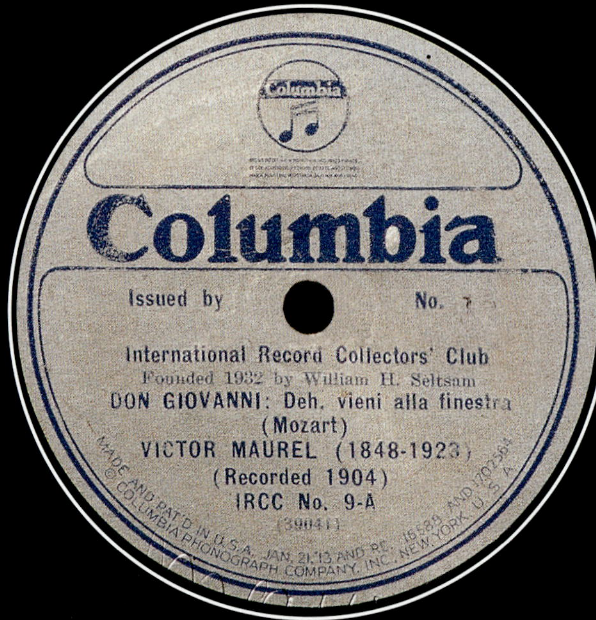

But soon there were Victor re-pressings as well. A number of the early ones were individually autographed by the singers themselves. The Emma Eames, shown here, was the only reissue that she ever autographed . . .

That many of the great singers of the turn of the century recorded we owe to the interest and enterprise of a young singer of the day whose name was Emilio de Gogorza. As a young man and young singer at the end of the 19th century, he acquired an interest in the phonograph, which he retained for the rest of his life. In the earliest days, he made records under various names, such as Señor Francisco, as became also a practice of the Gramophone Co. in its domain (in much of the rest of the world other than the U.S.), utilizing, for instance, the varied talents of Peter Dawson . . .

Also, in the first decade of the century, de Gogorza became an advisor to the Victor Talking Machine Co. It is beyond doubt that we owe it to him that certain singers made records at all. He himself continued as a prolific recording artist for three decades. He had the opportunity to record with some of the greatest of his day, such as his wife, the soprano Emma Eames. And he also made memorable records with Sembrich (see Archive Series VB29, and Caruso, VB58) . . .

Probably he was one of the greatest singers ever to have recorded; the critic W.J. Henderson in 1926 characterized de Gogorza as "the supreme artist of them all."

By the mid-1930s, William Seltsam of the IRCC had ferreted out a number of rare and, in some cases, hitherto unpublished recordings. These appeared in pressings by the original manufacturers that were of very elegant appearance.

In Europe, the Odeon Co. began at about the same time a series of historical reissues . . .

Almost all of these also appeared in England, with a different label from the Odeons and pressed by Parlophone.

Somewhere around this time (the late 1930s), the IRCC began an arrangement with Carl Lindstrom of Berlin, who had become the possessor of the surviving Fonotipia and early Odeon masters. These were not labeled as sponsored by the IRCC, but sometimes there was a sticker affixed to the pressing to this effect . . .

As the war approached, a man in Chicago, William Speckin, established himself as a rival to the IRCC. His Lindstrom pressings were marked as from the 'Historical Record Society' (HRS).

Seltsam's great discovery, made in 1937, was of Lionel Mapleson's cylinder recordings from the Metropolitan Opera between 1901 and 1903. A number of the cylinders were transferred and issued over the next several years; most of them had gold labels. There were further issues later, but many collectors feel that the gold label series are the best-ever transfers from the original recordings.

The enterprise of the HRS continued unabated. Whereas most of the Victor pressings for the IRCC had silver labels with blue lettering, by and large those for the HRS generally had gold labels with red lettering. And, like many of the IRCC pressings from the '30s, so too quite a few pressings done for the HRS had labels that were signed and sent in advance to the factory. This Dinh Gilly was not pressed until long after he died (in 1940) . . .

In the late 1940s, Victor decided to do its own series of issues. They had gold labels and were pressed on red vinyl, and indeed rather lavishly got up . . .

The Columbia Co. did not proceed very far with anything similar.

From this time on, neither American Victor nor American Columbia was much interested in doing pressings for the IRCC, HRS, or some smaller operators who had come on the scene . . .

But the Gramophone Co. (EMI) in England was more co-operative. They pressed records both for the IRCC and the HRS. There was a series, A.B.H.A., and A.B.H.B., which had rich blue labels . . .

But the majority of the records pressed by EMI, appeared with white labels and gold lettering . . .

Eventually (around 1951), all of these white label issues by the Gramophone Co. were made generally available. This group of records is now commonly referred to as the Archive Series.

A number of popular previous issues were re-pressed in the Archive Series, for instance Patti's notorious La Calasera . . .

The same had been issued on the Victor IRCC in a quite early edition (around 1934).

Nonetheless, an enterprising successor, Addison Foster of Philadelphia, followed in the footsteps of Seltsam and Speckin, and he persuaded the Gramophone Co. (EMI) to do a special series for him that had mauve labels with gold lettering (often referred to as the 'mauve-and-gold series'). A large number of important records appeared in this series throughout the 1950s . . .

Addison Foster's enterprise had come to an end by about 1960. There followed more than a decade of hiatus.

It is hard to resist some special cases, though we have chosen to be very selective in this matter. In 1936 and 1937, the extremely interesting soprano Blanche Marchesi, then in her seventy-third and seventy-fourth years, respectively, had made, by the Gramophone Co., a number of records. These were, for the most part, issued by the IRCC, pressed by Victor with individually autographed labels. But the Gramophone Co. did some additional pressings with HMV labels, which Marchesi distributed herself. The two sides of one of these records are illustrated here.

In the 1970s, spearheaded by Richard Bebb with the continuing support of Desmond Shawe-Taylor, as well as encouragement from the Earl of Harewood, a new series was commenced in England. It came to be called 'Historic Masters' and continues up to the present. One hundred and fifty-six different discs will now have appeared, and surpass the quantity achieved by most of Historic Masters predecessors. Most of them have blue labels ...

... but a special series featuring recordings made in Russia prior to 1915 — an extraordinary cache — has pink labels. The pink label Russian series is the result of an outright gift from Dr. John Stratton. Some further issues have had black labels. Many of these have appeared through a generous subsidy by Richard Bebb, and a similiar subsidy by Dr. John Stratton.

None of the issues that form the substance of this book should be confused with the fairly large number of special pressings that are in collections. The Victor Co. had a list of available matrices in the 1920s, and copies pressed-to-order had individually typed labels . . .

The Gramophone Co. also offered (not very loudly) a special-pressing service, and, from the 1930s until about 1960, these pressings had HMV labels. One was allowed to order up to three copies at a time from a master, and the individual was left to fill in his own label.

PM 85061 Mattia BATTISTINI (b)
Un Ballo in Maschera : Alla vita (Verdi)
(877 c) -11-06 G. 052142
Un Ballo in Maschera : Eri tu (Verdi)
(886 c) -11-06 G. 052146

ODEON 'Meister des Gesanges' Series

Note : Though Issued earlier than the Parlophone series shown below much the same material was used. Therefore the appropriate Odeon (Od.) numbers for this series can be found with its equivalent Parlophone (PO) entry immediately below.

O 5 602 Pasquale AMATO (b)
La Traviata : Di provenza il mar (Verdi)
(XPh 3878) 2- 6-09 F. 92510 *PXO 81 rr*
Un Ballo in Maschera : Eri tu (Verdi)
(XPh 3925) 12- 6-09 F. 92509 *PXO 81 rr*
O 9 107 Dmitri Alexeyevich SMIRNOV (t)
Sadko : Hindulied (R) (Rimsky-Korsakov)
(21608) 15-10-29 Od. Electric O-9107
Ei uchniem (Folk) (R)
(21611-3) 13-11-29 Od. electric O-9107
O 4 786 (??) Conchita SUPERVIA (ms)
Carmen : Habañera (Bizet) (It)
(Pho 6053) (It) 17-10-27 F. 168102
Carmen : Seguidilla(Bizet) (It)
(Pho 6054) (It) 17-10-27 F. 168102

PARLOPHONE - ODEON HISTORIC SERIES

PO 61 Giuseppe ANSELMI (t)
Don Pasquale : Sogno soave e casta (Donizetti)
(XPh 2559) 22- 4-07 F. 62183
Od. 0- 5600
Luisa Miller : Quando le sere al placido (Verdi)
(XPh 2569) 25- 4-07 F. 62166
Od. 0- 5600
PO 63 Lilli LEHMANN (s)
Die Walküre : Du bist der Lenz (Wagner)
(xB 3147) 5- 7-07 Od. 50393
DST J IRCC P

Le Nozze di Figaro : Heil'ge Quelle (Porgi amor) (Mozart)
(xB 3150) 5- 7-07 Od. 50395

PO 69 Francisco D'ANDRADE (b)
Don Giovanni : Brindisi (Mozart)
(d'A 12E)* 1906 Lyrophone

* This matrix was re-numbered by Parlophon as 280 in their own series - was it dubbed ?? *Od. O- 9 928*

Adamo DIDUR (bs)
Il Barbiere di Siviglia : La calunnia (Rossini)
(XPh 3175) 23- 4-08 F. 74119
Od. O- 9 928

PO 76 Maria BARRIENTOS (s)
La Sonnambula : Come per me sereno (Bellini)
(XPh 1608) 12- 2-06 F. 39457
Od. 0- 5 601

La Sonnambula : Sovra il sen (Bellini)
(XPh 1609) 12- 2-06 F. 39458
Od. 0- 5 601

PXO 84 Emmy DESTINN (s)
Der Fliegende Holländer : Senta's Ballad (Wagner)
(xxB 5293) 1911 Od. 76916
Od. O- 9 030

Tristan und Isolde : Liebestod (Wagner)
(xxB 5300) 1911 Od. 80311
Od. O- 9 030

PXO 87 Alessandro BONCI (t)
La Bohème : Che gelida manina (Puccini)
(XXPh 366) 3-10-05 F. 74000 *IRCC C*
Od. O- 9 029

Faust : Salve ! dimora (Salut ! demeure chaste et pure) (Gounod)
(XXPh 1894) 22- 5-06 F. 74006
Od. O- 9 029

PXO 90 Mario SAMMARCO (b)
Rigoletto : Pari siamo (Verdi)
(XXPh 3369) 6- 7-08 F. 74132
Od. O- 9- 032

Riccardo STRACCIARI (b)
Zazà : Zazà, piccola zingara (Leoncavallo)
(XXPh 3840) 22- 4-09 F. 74171
Od. O- 9- 032

PO 93 Aino ACKTÉ (s)
Faust : Air des bijoux (Gounod)
(XPr -1-2) not known F. 39088 *IRCC A*

Lohengrin : Rêve d'Elsa (Einsam in trüben Tagen) (Wagner)
(XPr 4-2) not known F. 39089

PXO 104 Jacques URLUS (t)
Le Cid : Ah ! tout e bien fini (Ô souverain !) (Massenet)
(xxB 7046-3) 25- 1-27 Od. O-9 111
Lohengrin : In fernem Land (Wagner)
(xxB 7098-2) 25- 1-27 Od. O-9 111

PO 107 Giovanni ZENATELLO (t)
Otello : Ora e per sempre (Verdi)
(XPh 4049) 1-10-09 F. 92608
Od. O- 5 805
Giovanni ZENATELLO (t) Pasquale AMATO (b)
Otello : Sì pel ciel (Verdi)
(XPh 4070) 6-10-09 F. 92759
Od. O- 5 805

PO 108 Giannina RUSS (s)
Aïda : Ritorna vincitor (Verdi)
(XPh 400 A) 28-10-05 F. 39354
Aïda : O cieli azzurri (Verdi)
(XPh 400 H) 28-10-05 F. 39355

PO 110 Francesco VIÑAS (t)
L'Africaine : O paradiso (Ô paradis) (Meyerbeer)
(XPh 170) pre 20- 2-05 F. 39134 *HMA 88*
Aïda : Celeste Aïda (Verdi)
(XPh 161) pre 20- 2-05 F. 39136 *HMA 88*

PO 119 Oreste LUPPI (bs) Ferrucio CORRADETTI (b)
Antonio MAGINI-COLETTI (b)
Crispino e la Comare : Di Pandolfini medici (1) (Ricci)
(XPh 481) 22-11-05 F. 39396
Crispino e la Comare : Puoi tornare al tuo panchetto (2) (Ricci)
(XPh 482-2) 22-11-05 F. 39396

PO 121 Rosina STORCHIO (s)
Don Pasquale : Quel guardo il cavaliere (Donizetti)
(XPh 1500) 2-12-05 F. 39400
IRCC V
Don Pasquale : So anch'io la virtù magica (Donizetti)
(XPh 1501) 2-12-05 F. 39401
IRCC V

PO 125 Adelina STEHLE (s) Edoardo GARBIN (t)
Adriana Lecouvreur : Ma dunque è vero (Cilea)
(XPh 95) (FD) 23-11-04 F. 39117 *HRS 1017*
Tadeusz LELIWA (t) Irene DE BOHUSS (s)
Chopin : Sera ineffabile (Orefice)

(XPh 105) (FD) 15-12-04 F. 39119

PO 127 Teresa ARKEL (s)
Les Pêcheurs de Perles : Siccome un dì (Comme autrefois dans la nuit) (Bizet)
(XPh 409) 30-10-05 F. 39361
Il Trovatore : D'amor sull'ali rosee (Verdi)
(XPh 411) 30-10-05 F. 39360

PO 128 Jean Francois DELMAS (b)
Les Huguenots : Bénédiction de Poignards (Meyerbeer)
(XPh 512) not known F. 39027 *HRS 1049*
Patrie : Pauvre martyr (Paladilhe)
(XPh 513-2) not known F. 39085

PXO 129 Giovanni ZENATELLO (t)
Otello : Niun mi tema (Verdi)
(XXPh 3371) 7- 7-08 F. 74103
Otello : Dio ! mi potevi (Verdi)
(XXPh 3372) 7- 7-08 F. 74104

PO 132 Salomea KRUSCENISCI (s)
Mefistofele : L'altra notte (Boïto)
(XPh 2212) 6-11-06 F. 39921
Adriana Lecouvreur : Io son l'umile ancella (Cilea)
(XPh 2213) 6-11-06 F. 39922 *HRS 1017*

PO 133 Antonio MAGINI-COLETTI (b)
La Danza (Rossini)
(XPh 443-2) 10-11-05 F. 39351
Carmen : Con voi ber (Votre toast) (Bizet)
(XPh 414) 2-11-05 F. 39374

PO 136 Eugenia BURZIO (s)
La Forza del Destino : Madre pietosa vergine (Verdi)
(XPh 4266) 20- 1-10 F. 62416
La Forza del Destino : Me pellegrina ed orfano (Verdi)
(XPh 4267) 21- 1-10 F. 62417

PO 138 Regina PACINI (s)
Il Barbiere di Siviglia : Una voce poco fà (Rossini)
(XPh 2053) 29- 8-06 F. 39783
Die Zauberflöte : Non paventar (O zitt're nicht) (Mozart)
(XPh 2059) 30- 8-06 F. 39777

PO 139 Oreste LUPPI (bs)
Mefistofele : Ecco il mondo (Boïto)
(XPh 258) (FD) 15- 5-05 F. 39206
Mephisto : Vergin bella ed adorata (Carelli)
(XPh 369) 4-10-05 F. 39314

PO 141 Giuseppe DE LUCA (b)

Il Barbiere di Siviglia : Largo al factotum (Rossini)
(XPh 2306) 14- 1-07 F. 39951
Il Trovatore : Il balen del suo sorriso (Verdi)
(XPh 2304) 14- 1-07 F. 39943

VICTOR HERITAGE SERIES

V. 15- 1000 Frances ALDA (s)
Otello : Salce (Verdi)
(C 8577) 25- 1-10 V. 88214
Otello : Ave Maria (Verdi)
(C 8578) 25- 1-10 V. 88213
V. 15- 1001 Luisa TETRAZZINI (s)
Le Nozze di Figaro : Voi che sapete (Mozart)
(2177 f) -12-07 G. 053145
Mignon : Io son Titania (Je suis Titania) (Thomas)
(2171 f) -12-07 G. 053142
V. 15- 1002 Mario ANCONA (b)
Faust : Dio possente (Avant de quitter ces lieux) (Gounod)
(C 4272-1) 27- 2-07 V. 88056
Un Ballo in Maschera : Eri tu (Verdi)
(C 4369-1) 3- 4-07 V. 88081
V. 15- 1003 Marcel JOURNET (bs)
Les Huguenots : Piff, paff (Meyerbeer)
(C 8552-1) 14- 1-10 V. 75146
Philémon e Baucis : Au brit des lourds (Gounod)
(C 8562-1) 15- 1-10 V. 74195
V. 15- 1004 Enrico CARUSO (t)
La Juive : Rachel, quand du Seigneur (Halévy)
(C 24461-2) 14- 9-20 V. 88625
Manon : Je suis seul ! ... Ah, fuyez, douce image (Massenet)
(C 11422-1) 27-12-11 V. 88348
V. 15- 1005 Pasquale AMATO (b)
I Due Foscari : Prenci ... O vecchio cor che batti (Verdi)
(C 13124-2) 14- 4-13 V. 88438
Germania : Ferito prigionier (Franchetti)
(C 13125-1) 14- 4-13 V. 88437
V. 15- 1006 Celestina BONINSEGNA (s)
Aïda : Qui Radames verrà ... O patria mia (Verdi)
(1952 c) 2- 4-09 G. 053232
Un Ballo in Maschera : Ma dall'arido stelo divulsa (Verdi)
(538 c) 1905 G. 053065

V. 15- 1007 Pol PLANÇON (bs)
Die Zauberflöte : Invocation : Possente numi (O Isis und Osiris) (Mozart)
(C-2201-1) 24- 1-05 V. 6371
La Lazzarone (Ferrari)
Le Fillibuster (Georges)
(C-2323-1) 20- 2-05 V. 85066 *IRCC 94*
V. 15- 1008 Jeanne GERVILLE-RÉACHE (ms)
Carmen : Habañera (Bizet)
(C 8334-1) 9-12-10 V. 88278
Paul et Virginie : Chanson du Tigre (Massé)
(C 9700-2) 5- 5-11 V. 88317 *IRCC 73*
V. 15- 1009 John McCORMACK (t) Mario SAMMARCO (b)
La Bohème : O Mimì tu più non torni (Puccini)
(C 8737-1) 23- 3-10 V. 89044
Lucrezia BORI (s) John McCORMACK (t)
La Traviata : Parigi o cara (Verdi)
(C 14686-1) 8- 4-14 V. 88453
V. 15- 1010 Mattia BATTISTINI (b)
La Favorite : A tanto amor (Pour tant d'amour) (Donizetti)
(884 c) -11-06 G. 052144
Martha : Povero Lionello ... Il mio Lionello (Flotow)
(833 c) -11-06 G. 052143
V. 15- 1011 Louise HOMER (ms)
Les Huguenots : Nobil Signori (Nobil Siegneurs, salut !) (Meyerbeer)
(C 490-2) 6-10-03 V. 85005
Die Allmacht (Schubert)
not known V. 88231
V. 15- 1012 Ernestine SCHUMANN-HEINK (c)
Lucrezia Borgia : Trinklied (Il segreto) (G) (Donizetti)
(C 2978-1) 3- 1-06 V. 85096
Leggiero invisibile (Bolero) (La Gitana) (Arditi)
(C 4701-1) 24- 7-07 V. 88093
V. 15- 1013 Charles DALMORÈS (t)
Roméo et Juliette : Ah lève-toi, soleil (Gounod)
(C 12537-1) V. 85121
Carmen : La fleur que tu m'avais jetée (Bizet)
(C 4249-3) 24-10-12 V. 85122 *IRCC 24*
V. 15- 1014 Emmy DESTINN (s)
La Gioconda : Suicidio (Ponchielli)
(C 14509-2) 9- 4-14 V. 88478
Madama Butterfly : Piangi, perchè ? ... Un bel dì vedremo (Puccini)
(0801 v) 1908 G. 053171
V. 15- 1015 John McCORMACK (t)

Don Giovanni : Il mio tesoro (Mozart)
(C 17647-1) 9- 5-16 V. 74484
La Fille du Regiment : Per viver vicino a Maria (Donizetti)
(C 8739-1) 23- 3-10 V. 88245

V. 15- 1016 Blanche ARRAL (s)
I Lombardi (Jérusalem) : Polonaise (Quelle ivresse)) (Verdi)
- 5-09 V. 74146 *IRCC 19*
Faust : Air des bijoux (Gounod)
- 5-09 V. 74147

V. 15- 1017 NOT FOUND

V. 15 1018 Mario SAMMARCO (b)
L'Africaine : Adamastor (Adamastor, roi des vagues) (Meyerbeer)
not known 1910-11 V. 88310
Hamlet : Brindisi (Ô vin dissipe la tristezze) (Thomas)
not known 1910-11 V. 88312

V. 15- 1019 Enrico CARUSO (t) Pasquale AMATO (b)
Luisa TETRAZZINI (s) Josephine JACOBY (c)
Rigoletto : Bella figlia dell'amore (Verdi)
(C 11447-4) 13- 2-12 V. Unp. G. 2-054038
IRCC 36
John McCORMACK (t) Dame Nellie MELBA (s)
Mario SAMMARCO (b)
Faust : Alerte ! Alerte ! ou vous êtes perdus (Gounod)
(4190 f) 11- 5-10 G. Unpub. *IRCC 7*

V. 15- 1020 Frieda HEMPEL (s) (s) Pasquale AMATO (b)
La Traviata : Dite alla giovine (Verdi)
(C 14716-2) 16- 4-14 V. 89079
La Traviata : Imponete (Verdi)
(C 14717-2) 16- 4-14 V. 89081

V. 15- 1021 Maurice RENAUD (b)
Hérodiade : Vision fugitive (Massenet)
(878 i) 15-10-08 V. 92003
Roi de Lahore : Promesse de mon avenir (Massenet)
(874 i) 15-10-08 V. 92002

V. 15- 1022 Janet SPENCER (c)
Don Carlos : O don fatale (O don fatal) (Verdi)
not known V. 74253
Hills o' Syke : (McLennan - Harris)
not known V. 74291

V. 15- 1023 Olimpia BORONAT (s)
Don Pasquale : So anchio la virtù magica (Donizetti)
(1506½ c) 1908 G. 053185
Rigoletto : Tutte le feste al tempio (Verdi)

(1507 c) 1908 G. 053186

V. 15- 1024 Fernando DE LUCIA (t)

Mignon : Addio Mignon (Adieu, Mignon) (Thomas)

(549 c) 1905 G. 052111 *IRCC F*

La Traviata : De' miei bollenti spiriti (Verdi)

(622 c) 1906 G. 052129 *IRCC 24*

V. 15- 1025 Enrico CARUSO (t) Louise HOMER (ms)

Aïda : Già i sacerdoti adunasi (Verdi)

(C 9748-1) 29-12-10 V. 89050

Aïda : Misero appien mi festi ... Aïda a me togliesti (Verdi)

(C 9749-1) 29-12-10 V. 89051

V. 15- 1026 Marcel JOURNET (bs) Louis DUPOY (b)

La Favorite :Anathème de Balthazar (Donizetti)

(01091 v) 11- 6-09 G. 034076

Marcel JOURNET (bs)

Le Chalet : Chanson Militaire (Adam)

(C 8541-2) 16- 1-12 V. 74281

V. 15- 1027 Marcella SEMBRICH (s)

Ernani : Ernani involami ... Tutto sprezzo che d'Ernani (Verdi)

(C-3155 -3) 3-11-08 V. 88022

Linda di Chamounix : O luce di quest'anima (Donizetti)

(C 6574-1) 2-11-08 V. 88142 *IRCC 48*

V. 15- 1028 Titta RUFFO (b)

Don Carlos : Per me giunto (C'est mon jour suprême) (Verdi)

(1318 c) 1907 G. 052190

Dai canti d'amore : Siamo in maggio (E. Titta)

(464 aj) 3- 9-12 G. 052383

V. 15- 1029 Riccardo MARTIN (t)

Le Cid : Ah ! tout est bien fini ! ... Ô Souverain ! ô Juge ! ô Père

(Massenet)

(C 9695-1) 8-12-10 V. 88316 *HRS 1002*

Cavalleria Rusticana : Ma prima voglio (Mamma quel vino) (Mascagni)

(C 9696-1) 8-12-10 V. 88277 *IRCC 17*

V. 15- 1030 Otto GORITZ (b)

Das Goldene Kreuz : Bombardon's son (Wie anders war) (Brüll)

(C 13237) 5- 5-13 V. 74342

Tannhäuser : Blick'ich umher (Wagner)

(C 9838-1) 23- 1-11 V. 74215

V. 15-1031 - 1035 NOT FOUND [[V. 15-1034 Plancon allocated but Unp.]]

V. 15- 1036 Enrico CARUSO (t)

Martha : M'apparì tutt'amor (Ach so fromm) (Flotow)

(C 3100-1) 11-2-06 V. 88001
La Favorite : Spirto gentil (Ange si pur) (Donizetti)
(C 3104-1) 11- 2-06 V. 88004

V. 15- 1037 Enrico CARUSO (t)
Les Huguenots : Ah, qual soave vision ... Bianca al par (Ah ! quel spetacle enchanteur ... Plus blanche) (Meyerbeer)
(C 8351-1) 7-11-09 V. 88210
Don Sebastiano : Deserto in terra (Donizetti)
(C 5008-2) 10- 1-08 V. Unp. 1st. Issue

V. 15 1038 Enrico CARUSO (t)
La Bohème : Io no he che una povera stanzetta (Leoncavallo)
(C 11276-1) 26-11-11 V. 88335
Macbeth : Oh figli, o figli miei ! ... Ah la paterno mano (Verdi)
(C 17197-1) 23- 2-16 V. 88558

V. 15- 1039 Enrico CARUSO (t)
Samson et Dalila : Vois ma misère hélas (Saint-Saëns)
(C 18821-1) 7-12-16 V. 88581
Nero : Ah ! lumière du jour ... Ah mon sort (Rubinstein)
(C 19485-2) 15- 4-17 V. 88589

V. 15- 1040 Enrico CARUSO (t)
La Danza (Rossini)
(C 11590-1) 13- 2-12 V. 88355
Fenesta che lucive (Cottrau - attr. Bellini)
(C 13107-2) 10- 4-13 V. 88439

V. 15- 1041 Feodor Ivanovich CHALIAPIN (bs)
Lakmé : Nilakantha's aria (Delibes)
(616 i) 7- 4-08 G. 022112
Faust : Il était temps (Gounod)
(2009 c) 29- 8-10 G. 022183

V. 15- 1042 Feodor Ivanovich CHALIAPIN (bs)
Norma : Ite sul colle (Bellini)
(613 m) 26- 4-12 G. 052353
Mefistofele : Son lo spirito che nega (Boïto)
(CR 388-1) 31- 5-26 G. DB.942

V. 15- 1043 Feodor Ivanovich CHALIAPIN (bs)
Boris Godunov : Monologue (1) (R) (Mussorgsky)
(CR 2130-2A) 4- 7-28 G. DB.1181
Boris Godunov : Monologue (2) (R) (Mussorgsky)
(CR 2131-1A) 4- 7-28 G. DB.1181

V. 15- 1044 Feodor Ivanovich CHALIAPIN (bs)
Boris Godunov : Clock scene (R) (Mussorgsky)
(CR 2134-1A) 4- 7-28 G. DB.1182
Boris Godunov : Farewell my son (R) (Mussorgsky)

(CR 2141-1A) 4- 7-28 G. DB.1183

V. 15- 1045 Feodor Ivanovich CHALIAPIN (bs)

Robert le Diable : Suor che riposate (Nonnes, qui reposez) (Meyerbeer)

(C 29246-1) 3- 1-24 V. Unp. 1st. Issue

Don Carlos : Dormirò sol (Je dormirai dans mon manteau royal) (Verdi)

(2021 c) 29- 8-10 G. 052292

V. 16- 5000 Enrico CARUSO (t) Frieda HEMPEL (s) Maria DUCHÊNE (ms)
Léon ROTHIER (bs) Andrès Perellò DE SEGUROLA (bs)

Un Ballo in Maschera : Così scritto ... È scherzo od è follia (Verdi)

(C 14660-1) 3- 4-14 V. 89076

Enrico CARUSO (t) Luisa TETRAZZINI (s) Angelo BADA (t)
Josephine JACOBY (ms) Pasquale AMATO (b)
Marcel JOURNET (bs)

Lucia di Lammermoor : Chi mi frena (Donizetti)

(C 11446-3) 19- 1-12 V. 96201

V. 16- 5001 Enrico CARUSO (t) Geraldine FARRAR (s)
Gina CIAPARELLI-VIAFORA (s) Antonio SCOTTI (b)

La Bohème : Addio, dolce svegliare (Puccini)

(C 6025-1) 10- 3-08 V. 96002

Enrico CARUSO (t) Marcella SEMBRICH (s)
Gina SEVERINA (ms) Antonio SCOTTI (b)

Rigoletto : Bella figlia dell'amore (Verdi)

(C 5053-3) 7- 2-08 V. 96001

V. 16- 5002 Enrico CARUSO (t) Frances ALDA (s)
Marcel JOURNET (bs)

I Lombardi : Qual voluttà trascorrere (Verdi)

(C 11441-1) 7- 1-12 V. 95211

Enrico CARUSO (t) Frances ALDA (s)
Josephine JACOBY (ms)Marcel JOURNET (bs)

Martha : T'ho raggiunta ... Dormi pur, ma il mio riposo (Flotow)

(C 11440-1) 7- 1-12 V. 95210

V. 16- 5003 Enrico CARUSO (t) Geraldine FARRAR (s)
Marcel JOURNET (bs)

Faust : Alerte ! Alerte ! ou vous êtes perdus (Gounod)

(C 8545-4) 16- 1-10 V. 95203 rr
G. 2-034002

Enrico CARUSO (t) Louise HOMER (ms)
Marcel JOURNET (bs)

Samson et Dalila : Je viens célébrer la victoire (Saint-Saëns)

(C 22575-2) 10- 2-19 V. 89088

THE ARCHIVE SERIES

VA 1 Antonio CORTIS (t)
La Cena delle Beffe : Ahi ! che tormento (Giordano)
(B 37873-3) 28- 3-28 V. 1240
La Cena delle Beffe : Mi svesti ! (Giordano)
(B 37869-3) 28- 3-28 V. 1240

VA 2 Selma KURZ (s)
Die Königin von Saba : Lockruf (Goldmark)
(Bb 6956-3A) 14-10-25 G. 7-43083
14 Volkskinderlieder No.4 : Sandmännchen (Brahms)
(Bb 6996-2) 16-10-25 G. 7-43084

VA 3 Leo SLEZAK (t)
La Dame Blanche : Komm, o holde Dame (Viens, gentille dame) (Boieldieu)
(690 r) 1905 G. 3-42460
Die Meistersinger : Fanget an, so rief der Lenz (Wagner)
(11129 u) 1907 G. 4-42095

VA 4 Maria GALVANY (s)
Mireille : Valse ((Ô légère hirondelle) (Gounod)
(4731 h) 1906 G. 53483
Celestina BONINSEGNA (s)
Manon Lescaut : In quelle trine morbide (Puccini)
(2144 L) -10/11-04 G. 53372 *IRCC 63*

VA 5 Mattia BATTISTINI (b)
Don Giovanni : Deh, vieni alla finestra (Mozart)
(442 z) 1902 G. 52666
La Forza del Destino : Egli è salvo (Verdi)
(BA 13-2) 24- 5-21 G. 7-52194

VA 6 Pol PLANÇON (bs)
Faust : Vous qui faites l'endormie (Gounod)
(1924 G (b)) - 5-02 G. 2-26635
Mario SAMMARCO (b)
I Gioelli della Madonna : Sono un demonio buono (Wolf-Ferrari)
(HO 116 ae) 28- 6-12 G. 7-52028

VA 7 Enrico CARUSO (t)
Mefistofele : Dai campi, dai prati (Boïto)
(2871 b) 30-11-02 G. 52348x
Mefistofele : Giunto sul passo estremo (Boïto)
(1787 b) 11- 4-02 G. 52347

VA 8 Amelita GALLI-CURCI (s)
La Danza (Rossini)

(BVE 59731) 28- 3-30 V. Unp. 1st. Issue

Manon Lescaut : L'éclat de rire (Laughing song) (Auber)

(B 19338-2) 5- 3-17 V. 64669

VA 9 Enrico CARUSO (t)

Hantise d'amour (Szulc)

(B 14357-2) 10-12-14 V. 87211

Luna fedel (Zardi)

(2882 b) -12-02 G. 52442

VA 10 Sigrid ARNOLDSON (s)

Mignon : Connais-tu le pays ? (Thomas)

(1294 r) - 6-06 G. 33612

Celestina BONINSEGNA (s)

Il Trovatore : D'amor sull'ali rosee (Verdi)

(2176 L) -10/11-04 G. 53375

VA 11 Olimpia BORONAT (s)

I Puritani : Qui la voce (Bellini)

(1775 L) 1904 G. 53351

Les Pêcheurs de Perles : Siccome un dì
(*Comme autrefois dans la nuit*) (Bizet)

(1777 L) 1904 G. 53353

VA 12 Enrico CARUSO (t)

Aïda : Celeste Aïda (Verdi)

(2873 b) 30-11-02 G. 52369x

L'Elisir d'Amore : Una furtiva lagrima (Donizetti)

(B 996-1) 1- 2-04 V. 81027

VA 13 Fernando DE LUCIA (t)

Lohengrin : Mercè, cigno gentil (Nun sei bedankt) (Wagner)

(2905 W (b)) 3-12-02 G. 52650 *HRS 1025*

Carmen : Air de fleur (It) (*La fleur que tu m'avais jetée)* (Bizet)

(2899 R (b)) 3-12-02 G. 52437 *HRS 1025*

VA 14 Geraldine FARRAR (s)

Manon : Obéissons quand leur voix appelle (Massenet)

(B 6654-2) 8-12-08 V. 87023

Il Segreto di Susanna : Via ! così non mi lasciate (Wolf-Ferrari)

(B 12923-1) 17- 2-13 V. 87136

VA 15 Mattia BATTISTINI (b)

Ancora (Tosti)

(445 z) 1902 G. 52669

Fernando DE LUCIA (t)

La Traviata : Ah sì d'un anno ... Un dì felice eterea (Verdi)

(2156 L) c. 6-10-04 G. 52080

VA 16 Titta RUFFO (b)

Chatterton : Tu solo a me rimani (Leoncavallo)

(9228 e) 26-11-08 G. 2-52686
Titta RUFFO (b) Andrès Perellò DE SEGUROLA (bs)
I Puritani : Suoni la tromba (Bellini)
(10906 b) 1907 G. 54360
VA 17 Lucrezia BORI (s)
Iris : In pure stille (Mascagni)
(B 15904-1) 16- 4-15 V. 87219
Così fan tutte : In uomini (Mozart)
(B 26471-3) 12- 5-22 V. 87346
VA 18 Mary GARDEN (s)
Across the Steppe (Gretchaninov)
(BVE 36733-11) 5-11-29 V. 6623
Carmen : Voyons ... En vain pour eviter (Bizet)
(BVE 57526-3) 5-11-29 V. 1539
VA 19 Olimpia BORONAT (s)
Martha : The last rose of summer (It) (Flotow)
(1778 L) 1904 G. 53354
Antonina NEZHDANOVA (s)
The Nightingale (Alabieff)
(7223 L) 1908 G. 2-23321
VA 20 John McCORMACK (t)
Le Portrait (Parkyns)
(B 13235-1) 2- 5-13 V. 64374
Sospiri miei, andate ove mi mando (Bimboni)
(B 13032-1) 28- 3-13 V. 64333 *IRCC 217*
VA 21 John McCORMACK (t)
Manon : Chiudo gli occhi (Le rêve : En ferment les yeux) (Massenet)
(B 12764-2) 3-1-13 V. 64312
Les Pêcheurs de Perles : Mi par d'udire ancora (Je crois entendre encore) (Bizet)
(B 12707-1) 11-12-12 V. 64305
VA 22 Leo SLEZAK (t)
La Muette de Portici : Cavatine du sommeil (G) (Auber)
(10853 u) 1907 G. 3-42886
Die Königin von Saba : Magische Töne (Goldmark)
(14585 u) - 5-09 G. 4-42361
VA 23 Marcel JOURNET (bs)
Ascanio : Enfants, je ne vous enveux pas (Saint-Saëns)
(BS 383-2) 16- 5-22 G. 7-32072
Monna Vanna : Je n'ai rien entendu .. Dis-la vite (Fevrier)
(BS 384-2) 16- 5-22 G. 7-32074
VA 24 John McCORMACK (t)
A child's song (Marshall)
(B 11816-1) 2- 4-12 V. 64253

My Lagan Love - Old Irish (arr. Harty)
(B 18751-1) 25- 3-10 V. 64154

VA 25 Feodor Ivanovich CHALIAPIN (bs)
Don Quichotte : Chanson du départ (Ibert)
(0PG 429-3) 13- 3-33 G. DA.1310
Don Quichotte : Chanson du Duc (Ibert)
(0PG 428-4) 13- 3-33 G. DA.1310

VA 26 Feodor Ivanovich CHALIAPIN (bs)
Don Quichotte : Chanson à Dulcinée (Ibert)
(0PG 430-1) 9- 1-33 G. DA.1311
Don Quichotte : Mort de Don Quichotte (Ibert)
(0PG 637-1) 13- 3-33 G. DA.1311

[VA 27 Sigrid Onegin rr]

VA 28 Maria DUCHÊNE (ms) César VEZZANI (t)
Samson et Dalila : Mon coeur s'ouvre à ta voix (1) (Saint-Saëns)
(0W 479-4) - 9-31 G. DA.4819
Samson et Dalila : Mon coeur s'ouvre à ta voix (2) (Saint-Saëns)
(0W 480-1) - 9-31 G. DA.4819

VA 29 Enrico CARUSO (t)
Tosca : E lucevan le stelle (Puccini)
(1790 b) 11- 4-02 G. 52349
La Gioconda : Cielo e mar ! (Ponchielli)
(2874 b) 30-11-02 G. 52417

VA 30 Enrico CARUSO (t)
I Pagliacci : Recitar ! ... Vesti la giubba (Leoncavallo)
(2875 b) 30-11-02 G. 52440
Cavalleria Rusticana : Siciliana (O Lola) (Mascagni)
(2876 b) 30-11-02 G. 52418

VA 31 Enrico CARUSO (t)
Non t'amo più (Denza)
(2877 b) 30-11-02 G. 52441
La mia canzone (Tosti)
(2879 b) -12-02 G. 52443

VA 32 Enrico CARUSO (t)
Manon : Chiudo gli occhi (Le rêve : En ferment les yeux) (Massenet)
(B 1001-2) 9- 2-04 V. 81031
La Mattinata (Leoncavallo)
(2181 h) 8- 4-04 G. 52034 *VA 53*

VA 33 Enrico CARUSO (t)
Manon Lescaut : Donna non vidi mai (Puccini)
(B 12945-1) 24- 2-13 V. 87135
Cavalleria Rusticana : Intanto amici quà ... Viva il vino (Mascagni)
(B 2344-1) 27- 2-05 V. 81062

VA 34 Enrico CARUSO (t)
Tosca : E lucevan le stelle (Puccini)
(B 998-1) 1- 2-04 V. 81028
Tosca : Recondita armonia (Puccini)
(B 999-1) 1- 2-04 V. 81029

VA 35 Enrico CARUSO (t)
Pourquoi (Tchaikovsky Op.6 No.5)
(B 18656-3) 3-11-16 V. 87271
Pour un baiser (Tosti)
(B 8343-1) 6-11-09 V. 87042

VA 36 Enrico CARUSO (t)
Die Königin von Saba : Magiche Note (Magische Töne) (Goldmark)
(B 6062-1) 7-11-09 V. 87041
Les Pêcheurs de Perles : De mon amie, fleur endormie (Bizet)
(B 18823-2) 7-12-16 V. 87269

VA 37 Enrico CARUSO (t)
Germania : Studenti udite (Franchetti)
(1782 b) 11- 4-02 G. 52378
Germania : Ah, vieni qui .. No, non chiuder gli occhi vaghi (Franchetti)
(1788 b) 11- 4-02 G. 52370

VA 38 Enrico CARUSO (t)
Germania : Studenti udite (Franchetti)
(B 8710-1) 14- 3-10 V. 87053 rr
G. 7-52013
Germania : Ah, vieni qui ... No, non chiuder gli occhi vaghi (Franchetti)
(B 8713-1) 14- 3-10 V. 87054

VA 39 Enrico CARUSO (t)
Parted (Tosti)
(B 14550-1) 9- 3-14 V. 87186
Over there (Cohen)
(B 22125-4) 11- 7-18 V. 87294

VA 40 Enrico CARUSO (t)
Nina (Tre giorni son che Nina) (Ciampi)
(B 23143-4) 9- 9-19 V. 87358
L'alba separa della luce l'ombra (Tosti)
(B 19484-2) 15- 4-17 V. 87272

VA 41 Enrico CARUSO (t)
Vieni sul mar ! (Folksong)
(B 23139-2) 8- 9-19 V. 87305
Tu ca nun chiange (de Curtis)
(B 23141-1) 8- 9-19 V. (87365) d.s. 958

VA 42 Enrico CARUSO (t)
Sérénade de Don Juan (Tchaikovsky Op.38 No.1)

		(B 14355-1)	21-1-14	V. 87175
		Sérénade espagnole (Ronald)		
		(B 14359-3)	9- 3-14	V. 87619
VA	43	Enrico CARUSO (t)		
		Scordame (Fucito)		
		(B 23152-1)	11- 9-19	V. (87395) d.s.1007
		Senza nisciuno (de Curtis)		
		(B 23149-4)	11- 9-19	V. (87396) d.s.1007
VA	44	Enrico CARUSO (t)		
		Pimpinella (Tchaikovsky)		
		(B 12805-2)	17-1-13	V. 87128
		Guardanno 'a luna (de Crescenzo)		
		(B 13105-2)	10- 4-13	V. 87162
VA	45	Enrico CARUSO (t)		
		Amor mio (Ricciardi)		
		(B 14356-1)	21- 1-14	V. 87176
		Cielo Turchino (Ciociano)		
		(B 15569-1)	7- 1-15	V. 87218
VA	46	Maria GALVANY (s)		
		Hijas de Zebedeo : Carceleras (Al pensar en el duñeo) (Chapi)		
		(10895 b)	1907	G. 53527
		Variazione (Proch - Mozart)		
		(10894 b)	1907	G. 53526
VA	47	Fanny HELDY (s) Marcel JOURNET (bs)		
		Thaïs : Baigne d'eau mes mains et mes levres (Massenet)		
		(BTR 3345-1)	7-11-27	G. 7-34015
		Fanny HELDY (s)		
		Thaïs : Ô messager de Dieu (Massenet)		
		(BTR 3351-1)	8-11-27	G. 7-33096
VA	48	Marie Louise EDVINA (s)		
		Thaïs : Qui te fait si sévère ? (Massenet)		
		(Bb 32-2)	2- 4-21	G. 7-33037
		Thaïs : L'amour est un vertu rare (Massenet)		
		(Bb 33-2)	2- 4-21	G. 7-33038
VA	49	Dmitri Alexeyevich SMIRNOV (t)		
		Il Tabarro : Hai ben ragione (Puccini)		
		(Bb 304-1)	23- 6-21	G. 7-52179
		Rigoletto : La donna è mobile (Verdi)		
		(Bb 100-2)	29- 4-21	G. 7-52175
VA	50	Jean-Emile VANNI-MARCOUX (bs)		
		Don Giovanni : Deh, vieni alla finestra (Mozart)		
		(BTR 3190-2)	12-10-27	G. 7-32133
		La Bohème : Vecchia zimarra senti Puccini)		

(BTR 3189-2) 12-10-27 G. 7-32132

VA 51 George BAKLANOV (b)

Eugene Onegin : There is no doubt (Tchaikovsky)
(B 22894) 1919 V. Unp. G. 7-22002

Don Giovanni : Deh, vieni alla finestra (Mozart)
(B 22877-1) 27- 5-19 V. Unp. G. 7-52136

VA 52 Bernardo DE MURO (t) Augusta OLTRABELLA (s)

Andrea Chénier : Ora soave (Giordano)
(BE 978-2) 12- 2-23 G. 7-54026

Andrea Chénier : Vicino a te (Giordano)
(BE 979-2) 12- 2-23 G. 7-54027

VA 53 Enrico CARUSO (t)

Fedora : Amor ti vieta (Giordano)
(2872 b) 30-11-02 G. 52439 *VA 58*

La Mattinata (Leoncavallo)
(2181 h) 8- 4-04 G. 52034 *VA 32*

VA 54 Jean-Emile VANNI-MARCOUX (bs)

Panurge : Touraine est un pays (Massenet)
(BF 3316-2) 28- 5-30 G. DA.1124

Fernand ANSSEAU (t) Tilkin SERVAIS (b)

(VA 54 rr) *La Muette de Portici : L'amour sacré de la patria* (Auber)
(BF 3304-1T1) 26- 5-30 G. E.560

VA 55 Titta RUFFO (b)

Sei morta nella mia vita (Costa)
(BVE 24109-3) 18- 2-29 V. 1460

Tizianello : Canto il grillo (Billi)
(BVE 49960-1) 15- 2-29 V. 1460

VA 56 Sigrid ARNOLDSON (s)

Il Barbiere di Siviglia : Un voce poco fà (Rossini)
(3579 r) 11-11-07 G. 53517

Carmen : L'amour est un oiseau rebelle (Bizet)
(1286 r) - 6-06 G. 33610

VA 57 Leo SLEZAK (t)

Louise : O gesang von Paris (De Paris tout en fête) (Charpentier)
(884 z) 1903 G. 2-42730

Leo SLEZAK (t) Elise ELIZZA (s) Grete FORST (s)
Hermine KITTEL (c) Gerhard STEHMANN (b)
Hermann WEIDEMANN (b) Ch.

Guillaume Tell : Dir Sonne Strahlt (Finale of opera) (Rossini)
(10862 u) 1907 G. 2-44241

VA 58 Enrico CARUSO (t)

Fedora : Amor ti vieta (Giordano)
(2872 b) 30-11-02 G. 52439 *VA 53*

Manon : Chiudi gli occhi (Le rêve : En ferment les yeux) (Massenet)
(1785 b) 11- 4-02 G. 52345

VA 59 John McCORMACK (t)
Desolation (Bantock)
(Bb 11336-1) 1- 9-27 G. DA.917
Dream of Spring (Bantock)
(Bb 11337-1) 1- 9-27 G. DA.917

VA 60 Hina SPANI (s)
Se Florindo e fedele (Scarlatti)
(BM 800) 4- 4-29 G. ER.320
Amarilli (Caccini)
(BM 798) 4- 4-29 G. ER.320

VA 61 Giovanni MARTINELLI (t)
Werther : Pourquoi me réveiller (Massenet)
(B 21430-4) 14- 2-18 V. 64774
Ouvre ton coeur (Bizet)
(B 17384-3) 28- 3-16 V. 64574

VA 62 Francesco TAMAGNO (t)
Hérodiade : Quand nos jours (Massenet)
(3027 b) - 2-03 G. 52684
Samson et Dalila : Figli miei (Arrêtez, ô mes frères !) (Saint- Saëns)
(3019 b) - 2-03 G. 52681

VA 63 Fernand ANSSEAU (t)
Monna Vanva : Elle est à moi (Février)
(BS 4260-1) 26- 9-29 G. DA.1064
Monna Vanna : C'est étrange (Février)
(BS 4259-1) 26- 9-29 G. DA.1064

VA 64 Elisabeth RETHBERG (s)
Der Fliegende Holländer : Senta's Ballad (1) (Wagner)
(BVE 58631-2) 30- 1-30 V. 1477
Der Fliegende Holländer : Senta's Ballad (2) (Wagner)
(BVE 58632-1) 30- 1-30 V. 1477

VA 65 Mattia BATTISTINI (b) Lulu HAYES (s)
Rigoletto : No, vecchio, t'ingani ... Sì vendetta (Verdi)
(BA 8-2) 23- 5-21 G. 7-54018
Fernando DE LUCIA (t)
Don Giovanni : Il mio tesoro (Mozart)
(11166 b) c. - 5-08 G. 054043

VA 66 Dinh GILLY (b)
La Bohème : Vecchia zimarra senti (Puccini)
(Bb 3341-1) 22- 8-23 G. 7-52244
Il Tabarro : Scorri fiume (Puccini)
(Bb 3342-1) 22- 8-23 G. 7-52245

VA 67 Rosa PONSELLE (s)
Beloved (Silberta)
(BVE 32852-5) 5- 6-25 V. Unp. 1st. Issue
Sanctuary (The little old garden) (Hewitt)
(BVE 32850-2) 1- 6-25 V. Unp. 1st. Issue

VA 68 Rosa PONSELLE (s)
When I have sung my songs (to you) (Charles)
(PBS 042209-3) 31-10-39 V. Unp. 1st. Issue

(VA 68 rr) *Luna d'estate* (Tosti)
(BVE 35467-2) 18- 5-26 V. 1164

VA 69 Rosa PONSELLE (s)
La Spagnola (E) (di Chiara)
(BVE 32873-2) 5- 6-25 V. Unp. 1st. Issue
La Rosita (Dupont)
(BVE 32851-5) 4- 6-25 V. Unp. 1st. Issue

VA 70 Ezio PINZA (bs) Roberto D'ALESSIO (t)
La Favorite : Non sei tu (Sais-tu devant la tiare) (Donizetti)
(BE 1216-2) 20- 6-23 G. 7-54028
Ezio PINZA (bs) Aristodemo GIORGINI (t)
Faust : Ebben ? che ti pare (Eh bien ? que t'en semble) (Gounod)
(BK 1822-2) 19-12-24G. 7-54036

VA 71 Marcel JOURNET (bs)
Die Meistersinger : Rêve, rêve (Monologue Hans Sachs) (1) (Wagner)
(0G 838-2) 10- 6-31 G. DA.1229
Die Meistersinger : Un elfe a tout fait (Monologue Hans Sachs) (2) (Wagner)
(0G 839-2) 10- 6-31 G. DA.1229

VA 72 John McCORMACK (t)
Allerseelen (R. Strauss)
(Bb 11339-2) 1- 9-27 G. DA.932
Automne (Fauré)
(0B 3582-1) 16- 9-32 G. DA.1286

VB 1 Feodor Ivanovich CHALIAPIN (bs) Marie MICHAILOVA (s)
Faust : Seigneur, daignez permettre (Gounod)
(2008½ c) 29- 8-10 G. 024039
Fernando DE LUCIA (t) Josefina HUGUET (s)
Antonio PINI-CORSI (b)
Il Barbiere di Siviglia : Ah ! qual colpo (Rossini)
(630 c) c. - 5-06 G. 054083

VB 2 Selma KURZ (s)
L'Étoile du Nord : Là là là , air chérie (Meyerbeer)
(2068 c) 27-10-10 G. 043164

Lakmé : Glöckchenaria (Là bas, dans la forêt) (Delibes)
(575 m) 28- 9-11 G. 043182
(VB 3 rr) Rosa PONSELLE (s)
La Vestale : Tu che invoco (Spontini)
(CVE 35464-1) 18- 5-26 V. 6605
VB 3 *La Vestale : O Nume tutelar* (Spontini)
(CVE 35465-1) 18- 5-26 V. 6605
VB 4 Maria GALVANY (s) Francesco MARCONI (t)
I Puritani : Vieni fra queste braccia (Bellini)
(1446 c) 1908 G. 054208
Celestina BONINSEGNA (s) Luigi BOLIS (t)
Andrea Chénier : Vicino a te s'acqueta (Giordano)
(3205 c) 5- 6-17 G. 2-054075
VB 5 Amelita GALLI-CURCI (s)
Semiramide : Bel raggio lusinghier (Rossini)
(C 30905-2) 16- 9-24 V. Unp. G. 2-053235
HRS 1031
La Sonnambula : Ah ! non giunge (Bellini)
(C 30906-3) 16- 9-24 V. Unp. G. 2-053236
VB 6 Giuseppe DE LUCA (b)
Dinorah : Sei vendicata assai (Ah ! mon remords te venge) (Meyerbeer)
(C 29439-3) 5- 2-24 V. (74872) ds.6443
Benvenuto Cellini : (Recit) De l'art splendeur immortelle (Diaz)
(C 29438-3) 5- 2-24 V. (74873) ds.6443
(VB 7 rr) John McCORMACK (t)
Die Meistersinger : Morning was gleaming
(Morgenlich leuchtend) (Wagner)
(C 17656-1) 10- 5-16 V. 74479
VB 7 *Joseph : Champs paternels* (Méhul)
(C 20898-1) 23-10-17 V. 74564
VB 8 Giovanni ZENATELLO (t) Giuseppe NOTO (b) Luigi CILLA (t)
Otello : Questa e una ragna (Verdi)
(CR 501) 17- 6-26 G. DB.955
Giovanni ZENATELLO (t) Edouard COTREUIL (bs)
Otello : Niun mi tema (Verdi)
(CR 502) 17-6-26 G. DB.955
VB 9 NOT USED
VB 10 Pauline DONALDA (s)
La Bohème : Sì, mi chiamano Mimì (Puccini)
(687 c) 9- 7-06 G. 053104
Olimpia BORONAT (s)
Nightingale (R) (Alabief)
(1543½ c) 1908 G. 023041

(VB 11 rr) Gemma BELLINCIONI (s)
La Traviata : Ah ! fors' è lui (Verdi)
(CON 577 R) 1903 G. 053019

VB 11 Celestina BONINSEGNA (s)
Cavalleria Rusticana : Voi lo sapete (Mascagni)
(1430½ c) 1907 G. 053172

VB 12 Wilhelm HESCH (bs)
Die Meistersinger : Das schöne Fest (Wagner)
(268 m) 1906 G. 042133

(VB 12 rr) Pol PLANÇON (bs)
La Sonnambula : Il mulino, la fonte ... Vi ravisso (Bellini)
(C 870-1) 23-12-03 V. 85018 *IRCC 49*

(VB 13 rr) Dame Nellie MELBA (s)
Le Roi d'Ys : Vainement, ma bien aimée (Lalo)
(693 c) 7- 7-06 G. 03072

VB 13 Susan STRONG (s)
Die Junge Nonne (Schubert)
(2004 f) 1907 G. 043078 *IRCC 159*

VB 14 Mattia BATTISTINI (b)
Quo Vadis : Errar sull'empio (Nouguès)
(218 af) 27- 5-12 G. 052361
Quo Vadis : Amici, l'ora attesa e questa (Nouguès)
(227 af) 29- 5-12 G. 052365

VB 15 Luisa TETRAZZINI (s)
L'Étoile du Nord : Grand Air (Meyerbeer)
(HO 522 af) 26- 9-13 G. 2-053094
Semiramide : Bel raggio lusinghier (Rossini)
(4578 f) 2-11-10 G. 2-053034

(VB 16 rr) Enrico CARUSO (t)
L'Elisir d'Amore : Un solo instante (Donizetti)
(C 996-1) 1- 2-04 V. 85021 *VB 44*

VB 16 Aristodemo GIORGINI (t)
La Traviata : De' miei bollenti spiriti (Verdi)
(1490 c) - 5-08 G. 052240

VB 17 Giovanni ZENATELLO (t) Giuseppe NOTO (b)
Otello : Mio Signore (Verdi)
(CR 496) 17- 6-26 G. DB.953
Otello : Ora e per sempre addio (Verdi)
(CR 497) 17- 6-26 G. DB.953

VB 18 Mattia BATTISTINI (b)
Don Sebastiano : O Lisbona (Donizetti)
(885 c) -11-06 G. 052145
Mattia BATTISTINI (b) Emilia CORSI (s)

Don Giovanni : Alfin ... La ci darem la mano (Mozart)
(882 c) -11-06 G. 054104

VB 19 Leonid Vitalyevich SOBINOV (t)
Les Pêcheurs de Perles : Je crois entendre encore (R) (Bizet)
(1987 c) 6- 2-10 G. 022161
Manon : Le rêve (En ferment les yeux) (R) (Massenet)
(1981 c) 5- 2-10 G. 022139

VB 20 Maurice RENAUD (b)
La Damnation de Faust : Voici des roses (Berlioz)
(870 i) 15-10-08 G. 032094
Le Damnation de Faust : Devant la maison (Berlioz)
(876 i) 15-10-08 G. 032100

VB 21 Frieda HEMPEL (s)
Die Zauberflöte : Infelice sconsolata (O zittre nicht) (Mozart)
(545 m) 13- 4-11 G. 053260
Die Zauberflöte : Der Hölle Rache (Mozart)
(2386 c) 12- 9-11 G. 043185

VB 22 Frieda HEMPEL (s)
La Muette de Portici : Ô moment enchanté (Auber)
(2249 c) 24- 6-11 G. 033128
Die Entfuhrung aus dem Serail : Che pur aspro al cuore (Marten aller arten) (Mozart)
(719 m) 30- 5-13 G. 053326

VB 23 Mattia BATTISTINI (b) Emilia CORSI (s)
Ernani : Vieni meco (Verdi)
(880 c) -11-06 G. 054106
Mattia BATTISTINI (b) Aristodemo SILLICH (bs)
Ernani : Lo vedremo (Verdi)
(879½ c) -11-06 G. 054105

VB 24 Emmy DESTINN (s)
Rusalka : Rusalka's air : Lieblicher Mond (Dvorak)
(C 14757-3) 9- 3-15 G. 2-043016
IRCC 65
Lohengrin : Elsas Traum (Einsam in trüben Tagen) (Wagner)
(538 i) 1906 G. 043070

VB 25 Emmy DESTINN (s) Ernst KRAUS (t)
Lohengrin : Das süsse Lied verhallt (Wagner)
(542 i) 1906 G. 044057
Lohengrin : Wenn ich im Kampfe (Wagner)
(543 i) 1906 G. 044056

VB 26 Maria GALVANY (s) Aristodemo GIORGINI (t)
Don Pasquale : Tornami a dir (Donizetti)
(549 i) 1906 G. 054111

La Sonnambula : Son geloso (Bellini)
(548 i) 1906 G. 054112

VB 27 Francesco MARCONI (t)
Lucrezia Borgia : Di pescatore ignobile (DonizettI)
(1417 c) -10-07 G. 052200
Celestina BONINSEGNA (s) Luigi BOLIS (t)
Un Ballo in Maschera : M'ami, m'ami (Verdi)
(3204 c) 5- 6-17 G. 2-054071

VB 28 Celestina BONINSEGNA (s)
Norma : Casta diva (Bellini)
(216 m) 1904 G. 053050
Celestina BONINSEGNA (s) Luigi COLAZZA (t)
Ruy Blas : Ah, tu mi fuggivi ... O dolce voluttà (Marchetti)
(854 c) 1906 G. 054109

VB 29 Marcella SEMBRICH (s) Antonio SCOTTI (b)
Don Pasquale : Ma Brava ! Vado, corro (Donizetti)
(C 3181-2) 14- 3-06 V. 89002
Marcella SEMBRICH (s) Emilio DE GOGORZA (b)
Hamlet : Doute de la Lumière (Thomas)
(C 4871-1) 9-10-07 V. 89010 *IRCC 48*

VB 30 Edmond CLÉMENT (t) Marcel JOURNET (bs)
Robert le Diable : Du rendezvous (Meyerbeer)
(C 11468-1) 18- 1-12 G. 2-034015
IRCC 138
Robert le Diable : Le bonheur est dans l'inconstance (Meyerbeer)
(C 11469-1) 18- 1-12 G. 2-034016
IRCC 138

VB 31 Maria GAY (c)
Trovatore : Stride la vampa (Verdi)
(3803 f) 8-11-09 G. 2-053018
Samson et Dalila : Mon coeur s'ouvre a ta voix (Saint-Saëns)
(2154 f) -12-07 G. 033041

VB 32 John McCORMACK (t)
Wo find'ich Trost (Wolf)
(Cc 5029-1) 4- 9-24 G. DB.766
Du bist die Ruh' (Schubert)
(Cc 5030-2) 4- 9-24 G. DB.766

VB 33 John McCORMACK (t) Mario SAMMARCO (b)
Il Barbiere di Siviglia : O, il meglio di scordavo (Rossini)
(5205 f) 18- 7-11 G. 2-*054021*
IRCC 96
La Gioconda : Badoer questa notte ... O grido di quest'anima (Ponchielli)
(5206 f) 18- 7-11 G. 2-054022

VB 34 Fernando DE LUCIA (t) Josefina HUGUET (s)
Les Pêcheurs de Perles : Non hai compresso (Ton coeur n'a pas compris) (Bizet)
(621 c) c. - 5-06 G. 054082
IRCC 64
Carmen : La tua madre ... Mia madre io vedo ancor
(Votre mère ... Parle-moi de ma mère) (Bizet)
(1172 c) c. - 5-07 G. 054172

VB 35 Selma KURZ (s)
Le Nozze di Figaro : Deh vieni non tardar (Mozart)
(Cc 6992-2A) 16-10-25 G. 2-053250
IRCC 165
An dem schönen blauen Donau (J. Strauss)
(Cc 6973-2) 15-10-25 G. 2-043045
IRCC 165

VB 36 Maria NEMETH (s)
Die Königin von Saba : Der Freund ist dein (Goldmark)
(CA 101-1) 25- 6-29 G. D 1720
Die Königin von Saba : Doch eh' ichin des Todes Tal (Goldmark)
(CA 102-1) 25- 6-29 G. D.1720

VB 37 Antonina NEZHDANOVA (s)
Die Zauberflöte : Aria (Der Holle Rache) (R) (Mozart)
(2590 c) 17- 4-12 G. 023101
Wintermärchen : Schmücket euch mit Rosen (Goldmark)
(1931 c) 28- 1-10 G. 023052

VB 38 Dmitri Alexeyevich SMIRNOV (t)
Mefistofele : Giunto sul passo estremo (Boïto)
(2058 c) 12-10-10 G. 052293
Roméo et Juliette : Ah ! lève-toi, soleil (R) (Gounod)
(428 s) -11-09 G. 022133

VB 39 Dmitri Alexeyevich SMIRNOV (t)
Eugene Onegin : Faint echo of my youth (R) (Tchaikovsky)
(430 s) -11-09 G. 022154
May Night : Sleep, my beauty (R) (Rimsky-Korsakov)
(435 s) -11-09 G. 022155

VB 40 Dame Nellie MELBA (s)
Le Nozze di Figaro : Porgi amor (Mozart)
(Melba 26) - 3-04 G. 03028 *IRCC 34*
Adelina PATTI (s)
La Calasera (Yradier)
(684½ c) 1906 G. 03085 *IRCC 17*

VB 41 Luisa TETRAZZINI (s)
Les Huguenots : O vago suol (Ô beau pays de la Touraine) (Meyerbeer)
(HO 191 ac) 9- 7-12 G. 2-053071

HRS 1015

Crispino e la Comare : Io non sono più l'Annetta (Ricci)
(HO 520 af) 26- 9-13 G. 2-053093

VB 42 Giovanni MARTINELLI (t)
Samson et Dalila : Arrêtez, ô mes frères ! (1) (Saint-Saëns)
(CVE 49714-2) 7- 2-29 V. 8159
Samson et Dalila : L'as-tu donc oublié (2) (Saint-Saëns)
(CVE 497-2) 7- 2-29 V. 8159

Maria GAY (s) Giovanni ZENATELLO (t)
VB 43*Carmen : Sei tu ? (C'est toi ? C'est moi)* (1) (Bizet)
(CVE 59806-2) 12- 3-30 V. 7314
Carmen : No, mai Carmen non cedere (Jamais Carmen ne cedera !) (2) (Bizet)
(CVE 59805-1) 12- 3-30 V. 7314

VB 44 Enrico CARUSO (t)
Les Pêcheurs de Perles : Mi par d'udire ancora (Je crois entendre encore) (Bizet)
(268 i) 8- 4-04 G. 052066 *IRCC 61*
L'Elisir d'Amore : Un solo instane i palpiti (Donizetti)
(C 996-1) 1- 2-04 V. 85021 *VB 16 rr*

VB 45 Leonid Vitalyevich SOBINOV (t)
Rusalka : Unwillingly to these sad shores (R) (Dargomizhsky)
(2513 c) 30-10-11 G. 02242
Rafael : My heart trembles (R) (Arensky)
(2217 c) 27- 2-11 G. 022200

VB 46 Beniamino GIGLI (t) Nerina BALDISSERI (s)
L'Amico Fritz : Suzel, buon dì (1) (Mascagni)
(1051 aj) -12-19 G. 2-054107
L'Amico Fritz : Tutto tace (2) (Mascagni)
(1052 aj) 12-19 G. 2-054108

VB 47 Elisabeth SCHUMANN (s)
Der Hirt auf dem Felsen (Schubert) (1)
(2EA 5442) 21- 9-37 G. DB.3317
Der Hirt auf dem Felsen (Schubert) (2)
(2EA 5443) 21- 9-37 G. DB.3317

VB 48 Selma KURZ (s)
Les Vêpres Siciliennes : Mercè diletti amici (Merci, Compagnons) (Verdi)
(572 m) 27- 9-11 G. 053276
La Jolie Fille de Perth : Ah ... Deh vieni (Ballade) (Bizet)
(HO 680 m) 3- 1-13 G. 2-053077

VB 49 Mattia BATTISTINI (b) Maria MOSCISCA (s)
Linda di Chamounix: Un buon servo (Donizetti)
(224 af) 28- 5-12 G. 054393
Linda di Chamounix: Ambo nati (Donizetti)
(217 af) 25- 5-12 G. 052360

VB 50 Miguel FLETA (t) Emilio SAGI-BARBA (b)
Marina : Brindisi : A beber (Arrieta)
(CJ 620-2) 18- 3-27 G. 2-064006
Marina : Duo Jorge e Roque : Feliz morada (Arrieta)
(CJ 619-2) 18- 3-27 G. 2-064005

VB 51 Dusolina GIANNINI (s)
La Forza del Destino : La vergine degli angeli (Verdi)
(CF 2425-2) 29-10-28 G. 2-053345
La Forza del Destino : Pace mio Dio (Verdi)
(Cc 15056-2) 17-12-28 G. 2-053344

VB 52 Johanna GADSKI (s)
Un Ballo in Maschera : Ma dall'arido stelo divulsa (Verdi)
(C 13185-1) 6- 5-14 V. 88496
Un Ballo in Maschera : Morrò ma prima in grazia (Verdi)
(C 13186-2) 6- 5-14 V. 88497

VB 53 Dame Nellie MELBA (s)
Lohengrin : Elsas Traum (It) *(Einsam in trüben Tagen)* (Wagner)
(4185 f) 11- 5-10 G. 2-053019

(VB 53 rr) Adelina PATTI (s)
Mignon : Connais-tu le pays (Thomas)
(682-2 c) 1906 G. 03083

VB 54 Hermann JADLOWKER (t)
Fra Diavolo : Meine Freunde sind hier ganz im Still
(J'ai revu nos amis) (Auber)
(1179 s) 23- 9-13 G. 042435
Il Barbiere di Siviglia : Ecco ridente in cielo (Rossini)
(253 al) 26- 9-12 G. 052385

VB 55 Enrico CARUSO (t)
Don Pasquale : Com' è gentil (Donizetti)
(C 2340-1) 27- 2-05 V. 85048
La Partida (Alvarez)
(C 14661-2) 3- 4-14 V. Unp. G. 2-062003

VB 56 Enrico CARUSO (t)
Il Duca d'Alba : Angelo casto e bel (Donizetti)
(C 15572-2) 7- 1-15 V. 88516
El milagro de la Virgen : Flores purisimas (Chapi)
(C 14662-1) 3- 4-14 V. (88671)
G. 2-062002

VB 57 Enrico CARUSO (t)
Carmen : Il fior (La fleur que tu m'avais jetée) (Bizet)
(C 2341-1) 27- 2-05 V. 85049
Les Huguenots : Ah, qual soave vision ... Bianca al par
(Ah ! quel spectacle enchanteur ... Plus blanche) (Meyerbeer)

(C 2342-1) 27- 2-05 V. 85056

VB 58 Enrico CARUSO (t)
La Partida (Alvarez)
(C 22122-1) 10- 7-18 V. (88670) d.s.6458
Enrico CARUSO (t) Emilio DE GOGORZA (b)
A la luz de la luna (Anton)
(C 21773-2) 16- 4-18 V. 89083

VB 59 Enrico CARUSO (t)
Chanson de juin (Godard Op.102 No.6)
(C 18658-1) 3-11-16 V. 88579
Uocchie celeste (de Crescenzo)
(C 19483-2) 15- 4-17 V. 88587

VB 60 Enrico CARUSO (t)
Eternamente (Mascheroni)
(C 11271-1) 19-11-11 V. 88333
Lolita (Buzzi-Peccia)
(C 6032-1) 16- 3-08 V. 88120 rr
G. 062005

VB 61 Enrico CARUSO (t)
Manella mia (Valente)
(C 14358-1) 21- 1-14 V. 88465
Tiempo antico (Caruso)
(C 17343-2) 20- 3-16 V. 88472

VB 62 Enrico CARUSO (t)
Serenata (Bracco - Caruso)
(C 23151-1) 11- 9-19 V. 88628
I m'arricordo'e Napule (Gioè)
(C 24462-2) 14- 9-20 V. 88635

VB 63 Mattia BATTISTINI (b)
Nero : Epitalamio (Imen ! Imen !) (Rubinstein)
(235 af) 30- 5-12 G. 052370
Quo Vadis : O Febea (Nougès)
(219 af) 27- 5-12 G. 052362

VB 64 Dame Nellie MELBA (s) John BROWNLEE (b)
Un ange est venu (Bemberg)
(Cc 9551-1A) 17-12-26 G. DB.987
La Traviata : Dite alla giovine (Verdi)
(Cc 9550-1) 17-12-26 G. DB.987

VB 65 Amelita GALLI-CURCI (s)
Hamlet : Ai vostri giuochi (A vos yeux, mes amis) (Thomas)
(CVE 34232-6) 28-12-25 V. 6562
Hamlet : Ed ora a voi (Et maintenant écoutez ma chanson) (Thomas)
(CVE 34233-5) 28-12-25 V. Unp. G. 2-053257

VB 66 Amelita GALLI-CURCI (s)
Philémon e Baucis : Ô riante nature (Gounod)
(CVE 58128) 28- 3-30 V. 7658
Cantata con strumenti : Io vi miro ancor (Scarlatti)
(CVE 47428) 5- 9-28 V. 7658
VB 67 Maria IVOGÜN (s)
Ariadne auf Naxos : Grossmächtige Prinzessin (R. Strauss)
(2D 391-5) 4- 6-32 G. DB.4405
Ariadne auf Naxos : So war es mit Pagliazzo (R. Strauss)
(2D 392-4) 4- 6-32 G. DB.4405
VB 68 Maria GALVANY (s)
L'Incantatrice (Arditi)
(1399½ c) 1907 G. 053165
Maggio - Valzer (Duffau)
(1450 c) 1908 G. 053193
VB 69 Mattia BATTISTINI (b) Elvira BARBIERI (s)
Faust : Per di qua : (Morte di Valentino) (1)
(*Parici mes amis* (Chorus)) (Gounod)
(2817 c) 3- 6-13 G..054454
Faust : Stammi ad udir : (Morte di Valentino) (2)
(Écoutez-moi bien) (Gounod)
(2820 c) 3- 6-13 G. 054455
VB 70 Ezio PINZA (bs)
Lucia di Lammermoor : Dalle stanze (Donizetti)
(CE 1279-2) 11- 7-23 G. 2-052242
I Puritani : Cinta di fiori (Bellini)
(Ck 1817-2) 17-12-24G. 2-052280
VB 71 Fernand ANSSEAU (t) Marcel JOURNET (bs) Fanny HELDY (s)
Faust : Alerte ! Alerte ! ou vous êtes perdus (Gounod)
(CF 2995-2) 26- 2-30 G. DB.1609
Marcel JOURNET (bs) Fanny HELDY (s)
Hamlet : Doute de la lumière (Thomas)
(2G 840-1) 10- 6-31 G. DB.1609
VB 72 Feodor Ivanovich CHALIAPIN (bs)
Lucrezia Borgia : Vieni la mia vendetta (Donizetti)
(2693 c) 26-10-12 G. 052388
Ernani : Infelice e tuo credevi (Verdi)
(2694 c) 26-10-12 G. 052389
VB 73 Rosa PONSELLE (s) Giovanni MARTINELLI (t)
Aïda : Pur ti riveggo (Verdi)
(C 29446-2) 7- 2-24 V. Unp. *IRCC 126*
Aïda : Là, tra foreste vergine (Verdi)
(C 29447-2) 7- 2-24 V. Unp.1st. Issue

VB 74 Rosa PONSELLE (s)
Ave Maria (Schubert)
(PCS 042212-5) 1-11-39 V. Unp. 1st. Issue
Home, sweet home (Bishop)
(CVE 32866-2) 3- 6-25 V. Unp. 1st. Issue

RUBINI RECORDS (Syd Gray) (Phonotypes)

M 1816 Fernando DE LUCIA (t) Angela DE ANGELIS (s) 16- 9-17
Les Huguenots : Stringe il periglio (La danger presse) (Meyerbeer)
M 1820-2 Fernando DE LUCIA (t) Angela DE ANGELIS (s) 7- 9-19
Les Pêcheurs de Perles : Non hai compreso (Ton coeur n'a pas compris) (Bizet)

SYMPOSIUM (Phonotypes)
ALL Fernando DE LUCIA except where noted

A number of these may have been announced but not issued

M 1744 *Il Barbiere di Siviglia : Ecco ridente in cielo* (Rossini)
24- 5-17
M 1748 *Il Barbiere di Siviglia : Se il mio nome* (Rossini) 24- 5-17
M 1781 *Il Barbiere di Siviglia : All'idea di quel metallo* (Rossini)
w. Giorgio SCHOTTLER (b) 15- 7-17
M 1782 *Il Barbiere di Siviglia : Numero quindici* (Rossini)
w. Giorgio SCHOTTLER (b) 15- 7-17
M 1797 *Forza del Destino : La vita è inferno infelice* (Verdi) 5- 8-17
M 1798 *Forza del Destino : O tu che in seno* (Verdi) 5- 8-17
C 2507 *Vorrei* (Tosti) 23- 1-21
C 2511 *Oblio !* (Tosti) 23- 1-21
C 2558 *Manon Lescaut : Donna non vidi mai* (Puccini) 17- 4-21
C 2559 *Manon Lescaut : Tra voi belle* (Puccini) 17- 4-21
C 1745 *La Favorite : Una vergine (Une ange, un femme inconnue)*
(Donizetti) 24- 5-17
C 1752 *Manon : O dolce incanto ... Chiudo gli occhi*
(La rêve : Instant charmant ...En ferment les yeux)
(Massenet) 31- 5-17
M 1753 *Mignon : Addio Mignon ! (Adieu Mignon !)*
(Thomas) 31- 5-17
M 1757 *Mignon: Ah ! non credevi tu (Elle ne croyait pas)*
(Thomas) 31- 5-17
M 1756 *La Gioconda : Cielo e mar !* (Ponchielli) 31- 5-17
M 1763 *Aïda : Celeste Aïda* (Verdi) 3- 6-17

M	1772	*Aïda : La fatal pietra* (Verdi)	24- 6-17
M	1773	*Aïda : O terra addio* (Verdi)	24-6-17
M	1774	*Cavalleria Rusticana : Mamma quel vino è generoso* (Mascagni)	1- 7-17
M	1779	*Cavalleria Rusticana : Tu qui, Santuzza ?* (Mascagni) w. Angela DE ANGELIS (s)	1- 7-17
M	1780	*Cavalleria Rusticana : Ah ! lo vedi che hai tu detto* (Mascagni) w. Angela DE ANGELIS (s)	1- 7-17
M	1783	*La Forza del Destino : Solenne in quest'ora* (Verdi) w. Antonio ARMENTANO (b)	1- 7-17
M	1784	*La Forza del Destino : Le minaccie, fieri accenti* (Verdi) w. Antonio ARMENTANO (b)	1- 7-17
M	1785	*La Forza del Destino : Non si placa il mio furore* (Verdi) w. Antonio ARMENTANO (b)	1- 7-17
M	1792	*Luisa Miller : Quando le sere al placido* (Verdi)	29- 7-17
M	1815	*La Traviata : Invitato a qui seguirmi ... Mi chiamate ?* (Verdi)	2- 9-17
M	1750	*Mefistofele : Dai campi, dai prati* (Boïto)	24- 5-17
M	1751	*Mefistofele : Giunto sul passo estremo* (Boïto)	24- 5-17
M	1755	*Werther : Ah ! non mi ridestar (Pourquoi me réveiller)* (Massenet)	31- 5-17
M	1766	*L'Africaine : O paradiso (Ô paradis)* (Meyerbeer)	17- 6-17
C	1778	*L'Africaine : O Selika, io t'adoro (Ô ma Sélika)* (Meyerbeer) w. Angela DE ANGELIS (s)	1- 7-17
C	1789	*Il Guarany: Pery ! Che brami ? ... Sento una forza indomita* w. Angela DE ANGELIS (s) (Gomez)	29- 7-18
C	1790	*Il Guarany: Ah ! lo sguardo tuo ... Ma deh ! che a me* (Gomez) w. Angela DE ANGELIS (s)	29- 7-17
M	1808	*Le Roi de Lahore : Sia benedetto il dolore (Oui, je bénis)* w. Angela DE ANGELIS (s) (Massenet)	30- 9-17
M	1880	*Ave Maria* (Bach-Gounod)	20- 1-18
C	1881	*Sérénade* (Gounod)	20- 1-18
M	1758	*Les Pêcheurs de Perles : Mi par d'udire ancora (Je crois entendre encore)* (Bizet)	31- 5-17
M	1820	*Les Pêcheurs de Perles : Non hai compreso (Ton coeur n'a pas compris)* (Bizet) w. Angela DE ANGELIS (s)	30- 9-17
M	1765	*Cavalleria Rusticana : O Lola ch'ai di latti* (Mascagni)	17- 6-17
C	1767	*La Bohème : Che gelida manina* (1) (Puccini)	17- 6-17
C	1768	*La Bohème : In povertà mia lieta* (2) (Puccini)	17- 6-17
C	1788	*Fedora : Amor ti vieta* (Giordano)	29- 7-17
M	1800	*La Gioconda : Enzo Grimaldo !* (Ponchielli)	

		w. Antonio ARMENTANO (b)	19- 8-17
M	1801	*La Gioconda : O grido di quest'anima* (Ponchielli) w. Antonio ARMENTANO (b)	19- 8-17
M	1868	*Scetate* (Costa)	30-12-17
M	2114	*Serenade medioevale (Nell'alta notte)* (Silvestri)	6- 7-19
M	2103	*Voce 'e notte* (de Curtis)	24- 5-19
M	2104	*Torna a Surriento* (de Curtis)	24- 5-19
M	1760	*Tosca : E lucevan le stelle* (Puccini)	3- 6-17
M	1787	*Tosca : Recondita armonia* (Puccini)	19- 7-17
M	1818	*Lucia di Lammermoor: M'odi e trema ... Sulla tomba* (Donizetti) w. Angela DE ANGELIS (s)	30- 9-17
M	1819	*Lucia di Lammermoor : Ah talor del tuo pensiero ... Verranno a te sull'aure* (Donizetti) w. Angela DE ANGELIS (s)	30- 9-17
M	1844	*L'Amico Fritz : Ed anche Beppe amò ... O amore* (Mascagni)	1-11-17
M	2234	*La Bohème : Che gelida manina* (Puccini)	18- 1-20
M	2012	*Les Pêcheurs de Perles : Mi par d'udire ancora (Je crois entendre encore)* (Bizet)	1- 9-18
M	2342	*Les Pêcheurs de Perles : Del tempio al limitar (Au fond du temple saint)* (Bizet) w. Benvenuto FRANCI (b)	11- 4-20
M	1813	*Lucia di Lammermoor : Tombe degl'avi miei* (Donizetti)	2- 9-17
M	1814	*Lucia di Lammermoor : Fra poco a me ricovero* (Donizetti)	2- 9-17
C	2120	*Lucia di Lammermoor : Tu che a Dio* (Donizetti)	17- 7-19
M	1898	*Legenda Valacca* (Braga)	3- 2-18
C	2121	*A Suon di Baci* (Baldelli)	27- 7-19
C	2726	*Palumella, zompa e vola* (Cottrau)	11- 9-21
C	2727	*Nu mazzo 'e sciure* (de Meglio)	11- 9-21
M	1791	*Il Trovatore : Ah ! sì ben mio coll'essere* (Verdi)	29- 7-17
M	1811	*Ernani : Mercè diletti amichi ... Come rugiada al cespite* (Verdi)	2- 9-17
C	2018	*Salve Maria* (1) (Mercadante)	11- 9-18
C	2019	*Salve Maria* (2) (Mercadante)	11- 9-18
M	2223	*L'Elisir d'Amore : Una parola, o Adina* (Donizetti)	23-11-19
M	2224	*L'Elisir d'Amore : Chiedi al rio* (Donizetti) w. Angela DE ANGELIS (s)	23-11-19
C	2340	*La Gioconda : Enzo Grimaldo !* (Ponchielli) w. Benvenuto FRANCI (b)	11- 4-20
C	2341	*La Gioconda : O grido di quest'anima* (Ponchielli) w. Benvenuto FRANCI (b)	11- 4-20

C	2405	*Ideale* (Tosti)	12- 9-20
C	2407	*Malia* (Tosti)	12- 9-20
C	2409	*La mia bandiera* (Rotoli)	12- 9-20
C	2437	*La gondola nera* (Rotoli)	24-10-20
C	2562	*I Pagliacci : Serenata* (Leoncavallo)	17-4-21
C	2343	*Mefistofele : Forma ideal purissima* (Boïto)	18-4-20
C	2508	*Caro mio ben* (Giordani)	23- 1-21
M	1754-2	*L'Elisir d'Amore : Una furtiva lagrima* (Donizetti)	24-6-17
M	1759-2	*La Favorita : Spirto gentil* (Donizetti)	5-8-17
M	1770	*La Traviata : Un dì, felice eterea* (Verdi) w. Angela DE ANGELIS (s)	24-6-17
M	1771	*La Traviata : Parigi, o cara* (Verdi) w. Angela DE ANGELIS (s)	24-6-17
C	2344	*Mefistofele : Colma il tuo cor* (Boïto)	18-4-20
C	2452	*Iris : Apri la tua finestra* (Mascagni)	7-11-20
C	2345	*Aprile* (Tosti)	24-10-20
C	2459	*Ninon* (F) (Tosti)	7-11-20
C	2531	*Andrea Chénier : Colpito qui m'avete* (1) (Giordano)	6-2-21
C	2532	*Andrea Chénier : E volli pien d'amore pregar* (2) (Giordano)	6-2-21
M	2153	*L'Amico Fritz : Han della porpora* (1) (Mascagni) w. Angela DE ANGELIS (s)	5-10-19
M	2154	*L'Amico Fritz : Tutto tace* (2) (Mascagni) w. Angela DE ANGELIS (s)	5-10-19
M	1762	*La Traviata : Lunga da lei ... De' miei bollenti spiriti* (Verdi)	3-6-17
M	2117	*Otello : Niun mi tema* (Verdi)	27-7-19
C	2392	*Andrea Chénier : Come un bel dì di maggio* (Giordano)	15-8-20
C	2572	*Salomé* (Robert Stolz)	1-5-21
C	1918	*Rigoletto : Un dì, se ben rammentomi* (Verdi) w. Angela DE ANGELIS (s) Vida FERLUGA (ms) Antonio ARMENTANO (b)	6-4-18
M	1919	*Rigoletto : Bella figlia dell'amore* (Verdi) w. Angela DE ANGELIS (s) Vida FERLUGA (ms) Antonio ARMENTANO (b)	6-4-18
M	1794	*Manon : Io son solo ... Ah ! dispar, vision* (*Je suis seul ... Ah fuyez douce image*) (Massenet)	5-8-17
M	1802	*Lohengrin : Da voi lontan (In fernem Land)* (Wagner)	19-8-17
M	1879	*Pietà, Signore* (Niedermeyer attr. to Stradella)	20- 1-18

C 3148 *Marechiare* (Tosti) 24-9-22
M 1786 *Ruy Blas : O dolce voluttà* (Marchetti)
w. Angela DE ANGELIS (s) 15-7-17
C 1809 *I Puritani : Nel mirarti* (Bellini)
w. Angela DE ANGELIS (s) 2-9-17
M 1812 *Les Huguenots : Bianca al par (Plus blanche)* (Meyerbeer)
2-9-17
C 2456 *Amor fà morir !* (Rotoli) 7-11-20
C 2457 *L'Alba* (Rotoli) 7-11-20

Angeles OTTIEN (s)
2303 *La Traviata : Ah ! fors' è lui* (Verdi) 30- 3-20
2309 *Lucia di Lammermoor : Ardon gl'incensi* (Donizetti) 30- 3-20

Benvenuto FRANCI (b)
C 2338 *Don Carlos : O Carlo ascolta (Carlos, écoute ... Ah je meurs)*
(Verdi) 11- 4-20
C 2339 *Aïda : Quest'assisa ch'io vesto vi dico* (Verdi) 11- 4-20
2320 *La Traviata : Di provenza il mar* (Verdi) 7- 4-20
2322 *Lucia di Lammermoor : Cruda funesta smania* (Donizetti)
7- 4-20
2321 *Un Ballo in Maschera : Eri tu* (Verdi) 7- 4-20
2336 *La Gioconda : O monumento* (Ponchielli) 10- 4-20

Mafalda SALVATINI (s) Pasquale AMATO (b)
4596 *Aïda : Ciel mio padre* (Verdi) c. 1926

Pasquale AMATO (b)
4589 *I Pagliacci : Sì può (Prologo)* (Leoncavallo) c. 1926

In addition : Excerpts from the complete 'Rigoletto' ss. 3, 5, 12, 14, 17, 18, 28, 29, 30 (C 1910, M 1922, M 1777, M 2299, C 1796, C 1915, C 1918, M 1919).
: Excerpts from the complete 'Barbiere di Siviglia' ss. 6, 7, 8, 9, 10, 11, 12, 22, 23, 25, 27, 32, 33, 36, 37, 38 (M 1990, M 2337, M 1996, C 1945, 1948-2, 1949-2, 1950-2, M 1984, M 1985, M 1997, C 1966, M 1987, M 1988, M 1964, C 1965, M 1999)

HISTORIC MASTERS

HMA 1 Conchita SUPERVIA (ms)
Lullaby (Cyril Scott op.57 No :2)
(WLO 3007) 17- 3-32 Od. Unp. Ist.Issue
When I bring you colour'd toys (Carpenter)

		(WLO 3006-2)	17- 3-32	Od. Unp. Ist.Issue
HMA	2	Fernando DE LUCIA (t)		
		Serenamente (Barthélemy)		
		(13334 b)	21- 5-09	G. 2-52772 *IRCC 5001*
		A Surrentina (de Curtis)		
		(13339 b)	21- 5-09	G. 2-52774
HMA	3	Hina SPANI (s)		
		Seis canciones : Canción del Carretero (Buchardo)		
		(BM 1585-2)	17- 4-30	G. AV 32
		Dia del feste (Ugarte)		
		(BM 1584-2)	17- 4-30	G. DA.1226
HMA	4	Francesco TAMAGNO (t)		
		Il Trovatore : Di quella pira (Verdi)		
		(3012 FT)	- 2-03	G. Unp. Ist.Issue
		Otello : Ora e per sempre addio (Verdi)		
		(3025 FT)	- 2-03	G. Unp. Ist.Issue
HMB	5	Mattia BATTISTINI (b) Elvira BARBIERI (s)		
		Il Trovatore :Qual voce ... Mira d'acerbe lagrime (Verdi)		
		(2815½ c)	3- 6-13	G. 054452
		Il Trovatore : Conte ! ... Vivrà ! Contende il giubilo (Verdi)		
		(2816 c)	3- 6-13	G. 054453
HMB	6	Selma KURZ (s)		
		Ernani : Ernani involami (Verdi)		
		(2070 c)	27-10-10	G. 053254
		Il Trovatore : D'amor sull'ali rosee (Verdi)		
		(571 m)	27- 9-11	G. 053279
HMB	7	Dmitri Alexeyevich SMIRNOV (t)		
		Les Huguenots : Plus blanche que la blanche hermine (R) (Meyerbeer)		
		(2857 c)	15-10-13	G. 022338
		Carmen : La fleur que tu m'avais jetée (R) (Bizet)		
		(2689 c)	21-10-12	G. 022312
HMB	8	Dmitri Alexeyevich SMIRNOV (t)		
		Ruslan & Ludmila : There is a desert country (R) (Glinka)		
		(2853 c)	14-10-13	G. 022334
		Rusalka : Unwillingly to these sad shores (R) (Dargominsky)		
		(2854 c)	14-10-13	G. 022357
HMB	9	Eugenio GIRALDONI (b)		
		Otello : Credo (Verdi))		
		(Xph 1512)	12-12-05	F. 39446
		Otello : Era la notte (Verdi)		
		(Xph 1513)	12-12-05	F. 39445 *HRS 1018*
HMA	10	FELIA LITVINNE (s)		

Aïda : Grâce pitié (I sacri nomi) (Verdi)
(XPh 694) [1905] F. 39217 *IRCC S*
Cavalleria Rusticana : Voi lo sapete (Mascagni)
(Xph 675) [1905] F. 39052 *IRCC S*

HMB 11 Conchita SUPERVIA (ms)
La Damnation de Faust : Autrefois un roi de Thulé (Gounod)
(xxP 7314) 26-10-31 Od. Unp. Ist.Issue.
Faust : Il était un roi de Thulé (Gounod)
(xxP 7313-2) 26-10-31 Od. Unp. Ist.Issue

HMB 12 Jean Émile VANNI-MARCOUX (bs)
Cléopâtre : A-t-il dit vrai ? (Massenet)
(2W 595) 5-10-31 G. DB.4822
Hamlet : J'ai pu frapper ..Être ou ne pas être (Thomas)
(2W 594) 5-10-31 G. DB.4822

HMB 13 Maria NEMETH (s)
La Forza del Destino : Madre pietosa Vergine (Verdi)
(CA 78-2) 11- 6-29 G. ES.571
La Forza del Destino : Pace mio Dio (Verdi)
(CA 79-1) 11- 6-29 G. ES.571

HMB 14 Reynaldo HAHN (b)
Maid of Athens (Gounod)
(WLX 374-1) - 5-28 Col. Unp. Ist.Issue
Lucien FUGÈRE (b)
Louise . Voir naitre une enfent (Charpentier)
(WLX 646) 1-12-28 Col. Unp. Ist.Issue

HMB 15 Maggie TEYTE (s)
Belle lune d'argent (Hahn)
Les Papillons (Chausson)
(2EA 10317-2) 15-11-44 G. Unp. Ist.Issue
Les Temps des Lilas (Chausson)
(2EA 10316-2) 15-11-44G. Unp. Ist.Issue

HMB 16 Eva Plaschke VON DER OSTEN (s)
Lohengrin : Elsas Traum (Einsam in trüben Tagen) (Wagner)
(2295 c) 24- 8-11 G. 043196
Lohengrin : Euch Lüften, die mein Klangen (Wagner)
(2296 c) 24- 8-11 G. 043197

HMB 17 Giovanni ZENATELLO (t) Giuseppe NOTO (b)
Otello : Sì pel ciel (Verdi)
(CR 499) 17- 6-26 G. Unp. Ist.Issue
Otello : Dio ! mi potevi scagliar (Verdi)
(CR 500) 17- 6-26 G. Unp. Ist.Issue

HMB 18 Evgeniya ZBRUYEVA
A Life for the Czar : Vanya's recit & aria (1) (R) (Glinka)

(2921 c) 18-11-13 G. 023142
A Life for the Czar : Vanya's recit & aria (2) (R) (Glinka)
(2911 c) 14-11-13 G. 023141

HMB 19 Lotte SCHÖNE (s)
Manon : Gavotte (Obéissons, quand leur voix appelle) (Massenet)
(CLR 5349) 6- 5-29 G. EJ 669
Manon : Adieu notre petite table (Massenet)
(CLR 5348) 6- 5-29 G. EJ 669

HMB 20 Olimpia BORONAT (s)
Ave Maria (Bach-Gounod)
(1544½ c) 1908 G. 053190x
I Puritani : Qui la voce (Bellini)
(1505 c) 1908 G.053282

HMB 21 Tito SCHIPA (s)
Manon : Ah, dispar, vision (Ah, fuyez douce image) (Massenet)
(722 aj) 10-11-13 G. 052421
La Bohème : Che gelida manina (Puccini)
(731 aj) 14-11-13 G. 052422

HMB 22 Selma KURZ (s)
Don Carlos : Tu che le vanità (Toi qui sus le néant) (Verdi)
(772 m) 19- 5-14 G. Unp .(053333) Ist.Issue
Les Diamants de la Couronne : Air & Variations (Auber)
(771 m) 19- 5-14 G. Unp. Ist.Issue

HMB 23 Luisa TETRAZZINI (s)
La Forza del Destino : Cruda sventura (Pace mio Dio) (Verdi)
(HO 547 c) 20- 6-14 G. Unp. Ist.Issue
Faust : Jewel song (Gounod)
(HO 552 c) 20- 6-14 G. Unp. Ist.Issue

HMB 24 Antonina NEZHDANOVA (s)
Il Barbiere di Siviglia : Una voce poco fà (R) (Rossini)
(2799 c) 20- 4-13 G. 023123
A Life for the Czar : I do not grieve (R) (Glinka)
(319 af) 13- 4-14 G. 023149

HMB 25 Lev Mikhailovich SIBIRYAKOV (bs)
La Juive : Si la rigeur (R) (Halévy)
(2030 c) 20- 9-10 G. 022173
Judith : Cease your grumbling (R) (Serov)
(2730 c) 15- 3-13 G. 022319

HMB 26 Vladimir Ivanovich KASTORSKY (bs)
Prince Igor : No sleep, no rest (R) (Borodin)
(403 m) 1908 G. 022126
Ruslan and Ludmila : Farlaf's Rondo (R) (Glinka)

(401 m) 1908 G. 022125

HMB 27 Elena Klimentyeva KATULSKAYA (s)
Vasili Petrovich DAMAEV (t)
May Night : Duettino Levko - Panochka (R) (Rimsky-Korsakov)
(2952 c) 9-12-13 G. 024092
Vasili Petrovich DAMAEV (t)
May Night : Levko's aria : Sleep my beauty (R) (Rimsky-Korsakov)
(1920 c) 24- 1-10 G. 022142

HMB 28 Dmitri Alexeyevich SMIRNOV (t)
La Traviata : De'miei bollenti spiriti (R) (Verdi)
(2062 c) 12-10-10 G. 022158
Manon : Chiudo gli occhi (En ferment les yeux) (Massenet)
(2844 c) 21- 8-13 G. 052416

HMB 29 Olimpia BORONAT (s)
Martha : Qui sola vergin rosa (Die letzte Rose) (Flotow)
(1515 c) 1908 G. Unp. Ist.Issue
Les Huguenots : O lieto suol (Ô beau pays de la Touraine) (Meyerbeer)
(1516 c) 1908 G. Unp. Ist.Issue

HMB 30 Graziella PARETO (s) Giovanni MANURITTA (t) Chorus
La Sonnambula : D'un pensiero (Bellini)
(Ck 1472-2) 10- 5-24 G. 2-054149
Francesco SIGNORINI (t)
Guillaume Tell : O muto asil (Asile héréditaire) (Rossini)
(1493 c) 1908 G. 052230

HMB 31 Clara BUTT (c)
Don Carlos : O don fatale (Verdi)
(2130 c) 19-12-10 G. Unp. Ist.Issue
Agnes NICHOLLS (s)
Oberon : Ocean ! Thou mighty monster (Weber)
(Ac 5840 f) 19-12-11 G. (03212 x)

HMB 32 Feodor Ivanovich CHALIAPIN (bs)
A Life for the Tsar : They guess the truth (R) (Glinka)
(312 af) 4- 4-14 G. Unp. Ist.Issue
Aufenhalt (R) (Schubert)
(310 af) 4- 4-14 G. Unp. Ist.Issue

HMB 33 Viktoria Viktorovna KAVETSKAYA (s)
Ihr Adjutant : Lied der Erna (R) (Winterberg)
(2434 c) 23- 9-11 G. 023083
Viktoria Viktorovna KAVETSKAYA (s)
Nikolai Fedorovich MONAKHOV (bs)
Ihr Adjutant : Duet Erna - Hennersdorf (R) (Winterberg)
(2433 c) 23- 9-11 G. 024055

HMB 34 Helene SADOVEN (s) Fernand ANSSEAU (t)

Werther : Oui, c'est moi ! .. (to '*Tout mon â me est là*') (Massenet)
(CL 45-2) 2-10-24 G. DB.783
Werther : N'achevez pas (Massenet)
(CL 46-2) 2-10-24 G. DB.783

HMB 35 Melanie KURT (s) Jacques URLUS (t)
Aïda : Ich seh' dich wieder (Pur ti riveggo) (Verdi)
(2138 c) 7- 1-11 G. 044173
Aïda : Entflieh'n aus diesem Lande wir (Fuggiam gli ardori inospitii) (Verdi)
(2139 c) 7- 1-11 G. 044174

HMB 36 Dame Nellie MELBA (s)
Distance Tests including part of : *Hamlet : Mad scene* (Thomas)
(4195 f) 11- 5-10 G. Unp. Ist.Issue
Francesco TAMAGNO (t)
Otello : Niun mi tema (Verdi)
(14 FT) - 2-03 G. Unp. Ist.Issue

HMB 37 Feodor Ivanovich CHALIAPIN (bs)
When the King went forth to war (R) (Koenemann)
(309 af) 4- 4-14 G. Unp Ist.Issue.
Ivan Vasilyevich GRYZUNOV
The prisoner of the Caucasus : Abukerer's aria (R) (Cui)
(1918 c) 24- 1-10 G. 022153

HMB 38 Lamberto BERGAMINI (t) Graziella PARETO (s)
Rigoletto : Signor né principe ... È il sol dell'anima (Verdi)
(3285 c) 9- 7-18 G. 2-054079
Graziella PARETO (s)
Rigoletto : Gualtier Maldè ... Caro nome (Verdi)
(3283 c) 6- 7-18 G. 2-053172

HMB 39 Melanie KURT (s) Jacques URLUS (t)
Aïda : Es hat der Stein sich uber uns geschlossen (La fatal pietra) (Verdi)
(2136c) 7- 1-11 G.044180
Aïda : Sieh' dort den Toresengel
(*Vedi ? Di morte l'angelo ... O terra addio*) (Verdi)
(2137c) 7- 1-11 G. 044181

HMB 40 Matteo DRAGONI (b)
La Forza del Destino : Urna fatale del mio Destino (Verdi)
(1151 aj) 17- 9-20 G. 2-052189
Germania : O pure visione (Franchetti)
(CE 287-2) 17- 4-22 G. 2-052222

HMB 41 Lydia Yakovlevna LIPKOVSKAYA (s)
Il Barbiere di Siviglia : Una voce poco fà (R) (Rossini)
(2727 c) 8-12-12 G. 023116
Il Barbiere di Siviglia : Io sono docile (R) (Rossini)
(2728 c) 8-12-12 G. 023117

HMA 42 Selma KURZ (s)
La Bohème : Leb'wohl ohne Hass (Donde lieta usci) (Puccini)
(10780 u) 1907 G. 43946
Parla (Arditi)
(9886 u) 1906 G. 53491

HMA 43 Francesco TAMAGNO (t)
Le Prophète : Sopra Berta, l'amor mio (Pour Berthe) (Meyerbeer)
(3015 b) - 2-03 G. Unp. Ist.Issue
Hérodiade : Adieu donc, vains objets (Massenet)
(3017 b) - 2-03 G. Unp. Ist.Issue

HM(A) 44 Celestina BONINSEGNA (s)
Te solo (Sabajno)
(9338 b) -10/11-06 G. 53492
Dame Nellie MELBA (s)
Jean (Burliegh)
(11689 e) 19- 5-10 G. Unp. Ist.Issue

HMA 45 Toti DAL MONTE (s)
Sei bella mia dolcezza (Schumann)
(Bb 6285-1) 2- 7-25 G. DA.720
Estrellita (Ponce)
(Bb 6284-3) 2- 7-25 G. DA.720

HMA 46 Feodor Ivanovich CHALIAPIN (bs)
Bolero (R) (Dargomizhky)
(0PG 431-1) 9- 1-33 G. Unp. Ist.Issue
Sapphische Ode (R) (Brahms)
(Y 16738 e) 5- 7-13 G. Unp. Ist.Issue

HMB 47 Mattia BATTISTINI (b)
Don Carlos : Io morrò, ma lieto in core (Ah je meurs) (Verdi)
(CK 1419-3) 24- 2-24 G. DB.737
Mattia BATTISTINI (b) Ebe BOCCOLINI (s)
Thaïs : D'acqua aspergimi (Baigne d'eau) (Massenet)
(273ai) 3- 6-11 G. (054318) Ist.Issue

HMB 48 Antonina Vasolyevna NEZHDANOVA (s)
La Serenata (R) (Tosti)
(2795½ c) 19- 4-13 G. 023125
Si vous l'aviez compris (R) (Denza)
(320 af) 14- 4-14 G. 023155

HMB 49 Hermann JADLOWKER (t)
La Muette de Portici : Barcarolle : O seht wie herrlich (Amis, la matinée est belle) (Auber)
(1181 s) 23- 9-13 G. 042436
La Muette de Portici : Schlummerlied : Du einz'ger Tröster

(Du pauvre seul) (Auber)
(1215 s) 20-10-13 G. 042437

HMB 50 Mikhail Nikolayevich KARAKASH (b)
Eugene Onegin : Onegin's aria A1 (*Written words)* (R) (Tchaikovsky)
(2878c) 25-10-13 G. 022344
The Queen of Spades : Yeletsky's aria (R) (Tchaikovsky)
(2744½ c) 22- 3-13 G. 022320

HMA 51 Titta RUFFO (b)
Visione Veneziana (Brogi)
(0B 5461-1) 25-11-33 G. Unp. Ist.Issue
Sei morta e la mia vita (Costa)
(0B 5463-1) 25-11-33 G. Unp. Ist.Issue

HMS 52 Anton VAN ROOY (b)
ss *Das Muhlrad* (arr.Erk)
(2012 FG (b)) 20- 6-02 G. 2-2700

HMB 53 Feodor Ivanovich CHALIAPIN (bs)
Demon : On the airy ocean (R) (Rubinstein)
(Cc 7193-1) 5-11-25 G. Unp. Ist.Issue
Demon : I am he to whom you listened (R) (Rubinstein)
(Cc 7194-1) 5-11-25 G. (2-022039) Ist.Issue

HMA 54 Conchita SUPERVIA (ms)
El Amor Brujo : Canción del Fuego fatuo (de Falla)
(So 6605) 13-10-30 Od.184201
El Amor Brujo : Canción del amor dolido (de Falla)
(So 6606) 13-10-30 Od.184201

HMB 55 Emmy DESTINN (s)
Die Zauberflöte : Ach ich fühls (Mozart)
(0820 v) 1908 G. 043097
Margarethe SIEMS (s)
Der Rosenkavalier : Kann mich auch an ein Mädelerinnen (R. Strauss)
(2303 c) 25- 8-11 G. 043179

HMB 56 Viktoria Viktorovna KAVETSKAYA
Under the lime trees (R) (Felix)
(2443 c) 25- 9-11 G. 023078
La Serenata (R) (Tosti)
(2444 c) 25- 9-11 G. 023079

HMB 57 Lev SIBIRYAKOV (bs)
Don Carlos : Elle ne m'aime pas (R) (Verdi)
(2047 c) 27- 9-10 G. 022176
Don Carlos : Je dormirai (R) (Verdi)
(2046 c) 27- 9-10 G. 022177

HMB 58 Evgeniya Ivanovna ZBRUYEVA (c)

Lev Mikhailovich SIBIRYAKOV (bs)
Boris Godunov : Marina - Rangoni duo - Will you permit ? (1) (R) (Mussorgsky)
(2905 c) 12-11-13 G. 024090
Boris Godunov : Marina - Rangoni duo (2) (R) (Mussorgsky)
(2906½ c) 12-11-13 G. 024091

HMA 59 Lilli LEHMANN (s)
Auf dem Wasser zu Singen (Schubert)
(xB 1304) 29- 6-06 Od. 50094 *IRCC Q*
Fidelio : Abscheulicher! wo eilst du hin ? (Beethoven)
(xB 3049) 22- 6-07 Od. 50356 *DST G*

HMB 60 Lilli LEHMANN (s)
Fidelio : Komm, Hoffnung (Beethoven)
(xxB 3050) 22- 6-07 Od. 80006 *DST H*
Fidelio : Ich folg'dem innern Triebe (Beethoven)
(xxB 3051) 22- 6-07 Od. 80007 *DST H*

HMB 61 Maria FARNETI (s)
Iris : Io piango (Mascagni)
WBX 1078-1 10- 8-31 Col. GQX 10326
Iris : Un dì ero piccina (Mascagni)
WBX 1079-1 10- 8-31 Col. GQX 10326

HMB 62 Julia CULP (c)
Der Lindenbaum (Schubert)
(CW 153-3) 29- 7-26 G. EJ.41
Der Tod und das Mädchen (Schubert)
(CW 154-1) 29- 7-26 G. EJ.41

HMB 63 Dmitri Alexeyevich SMIRNOV (t)
Tosca : E lucevan le stelle (Puccini)
(429½ s) -11-09 G. 052269
Meta SEINEMEYER (s) Carl Martin ÖHMAN (t)
Tosca : Hah ! Geleit für Floria Tosca (Franchigia a Floria Tosca) (Puccini)
(2-8583) 12- 2-26 Parl. P-2219

HMB 64 Meta SEINEMEYER (s) Carl Martin ÖHMAN (t)
Tosca : Wisse nah' ist die Stunde (Senti ... l'ora vicina) (Puccini)
(2-8584) 12- 2-26 Parl. P-2219
Tosca : Und sie kommen nicht (È non giungono) (Puccini)
(2-8585) 12- 2-26 Parl. Unp. Ist.Issue

HMA 65 Olimpia BORONAT (s)
Mireille : O d'amor messagera (Ô légère hirondelle) (Gounod)
(1773 L) 1904 G. 53349
Zabava Putyatishna : Guai ! No No ! (M.M. Ivanov)
(1774 L) 1904 G. 53350

HMB 66 Natalia Stepanova ERMOLENKO-YUZHINA (s)

The Guardsman : Little nightingale (R) (Tchaikovsky)
(2520 c) 31-10-11 G. 023090
Natalia Stepanova ERMOLENKO-YUZHINA (s)
David Kristoforovich YUZHINA (t)
Aïda : Fuggiam gli ardori inospiti (R) (Verdi)
(339 m) 1908 G. 024029

HMB 67 Maria FARNETI (s)
La Wally : Ebben ? Ne andro lontano (Catalani)
(WBX 1076-1) 10- 8-31 Col. GQX 10491
Madama Butterfly : Un bel dì vedremo (Puccini)
(WBX 1077-1) 10- 8-31 Col. GQX 10491

HMB 68 Eugenia Adalfovna BRONSKAYA (s)
Lev Mikhailovich SIBIRYAKOV (bs)
Les Huguenots : Tu m'as compris, adieu! (R) (Meyerbeer)
(285 af) 18- 1-14 G. 024098
Lev Mikailovich KLEMENTIEV (t)
Les Huguenots : Plus blanche que la blanche hermine (R) (Meyerbeer)
(406fl s) - 9-09 G. 022130

HMB 69 Mme Charles CAHIER (c)
Le Prophète : Ah ! mon fils (Meyerbeer)
(CS 2946-1T1) 20- 9-28 G. M.109 *IRCC 62*
La Favorite : Ô mon Fernand (Donizetti)
(CS 2947-2) 20- 9-28 G. M.109 *IRCC 62*

HMB 70 Evgeniya Ivanovna ZBRUYEVA (c)
Prince Igor : Konchakovna's aria : Now the day ! (R) (Borodin)
(2431 c) 23- 9-11 G. 023091
Khovanschina : Martha's song - In shame and disgrace (R) (Mussorgsky)
(2864 r) 1907 G. 2-23175

HMA 71 Germaine LUBIN (s)
Sylvie (Fauré op.6 No.3)
(0LA 4304) 25- 5-44 G. Unp. Ist.Issue
Au Bord de l'eau (Fauré op.8 No.1
(0LA 4305) 25- 5-44 G. Unp. Ist.Issue

HMB 72 Francesco MERLI (t)
Otello : Dio ! mi potevi scagliar (Verdi)
(CBX 1412) 25- 6-36 Col. GQX.10776
Otello : Niun mi tema (Verdi)
(CBX 1413) 25- 6-36 Col. GQX.10776

HMA 73 Elisabeth SCHUMANN (s)
Er laube mir, feins Mädchen-Wiekomm'ich denn (Brahms)
(0EA 6685-1) 8- 7-38 G. DA.1652
Heimkehr (R. Strauss op.15 No.3)
(0EA 6689-1) 8- 7-38 G. DA.1652

HMB 74 Evgeniya Ivanovna ZBRUYEVA (c)
From the shores of thy far distant land (R) (Borodin)
(2050 c) 1-10-10 G. 023066
Elizavyeta Fiodorovna PETRENKO (c)
Songs and Dances of Death : Serenade (R) (Mussorgsky)
(2055 c) 10-10-10 G. 023068

HMB 75 Richard TAUBER (t)
La Bohème : Wie eiskalt ist dies Händchen (Che gelida manina) (Puccini)
(xxB 6981-2) 25- 4-24 Od. LXX 80942
Madama Butterfly : O wie ich mein vergehen (Addio fiorito asil) (Puccini)
(xxB 7152-2) 7- 4-25 Od. LXX 76832

HMA 76 Maggie TEYTE (s)
L'Absent (Fauré)
(0EA 9877-1) 28- 5-42 G. Unp. Ist.Issue
Ce n'etaut pas la même chose (Ciboulette)
(0EA 11017-2 20- 5-46 G. Unp. Ist.Issue

HMA 77 John McCORMACK (t)
The Cloths of Heaven (Dunhill)
(Bb 11347-1) 2- 9-27 G. [6-2895]
Ein neues andächtiges Kindelwiegen (Trad-Comer)
(0EA 408-1) 24- 8-34 G. DA.1675

HMB 78 Adelina PATTI (s)
Ave Maria (Bach-Gounod)
(547 f) 2/12 12-05 G. Unp. Ist.Issue
Last rose of summer (Trad - Moore)
(546 f) 2/12-12-05 G. Unp. Ist.Issue

HMA 79 Andrei Markovich LABINSKY (t)
Dubrovsky : O give me oblivion (R) (Napravnik)
(4924 L) 1906-07 G. 3-22537
Mikhail Nikolayevich KARAKASH (b)
Don Juan : Serenade (R) (Napravnik)
(5768 ae) 16- 3-14 G. Unp. Ist.Issue

HMB 80 Vladimir Ivanovich KASTORSKY (bs)
Lakmé : Lakmé, ton regard se voile (R) (Delibes)
(402 m) 1908 G. 022127
The Two Grenadiers (R) (Schumann)
(424 s) -11-09 G. 022134

HMB 81 Natalia Stepanova ERMOLENKO-YUZHINA (s)
Norma : Casta diva (R) (Bellini)
(1935 c) 1- 2-10 G. 023045
Norma : Ah ! bello a me ritorno (R) (Bellini)
(1936 c) 1- 2-10 G. 023059

HMA 82 Giuseppe BORGATTI (t)

Lohengrin : Di, non t'incan (Atmest du nicht) (Wagner)
(XPh 1517) 13-12-05 F. 39407
Die Meistersinger : Nel verno al pie (Morgenlich leuchtend) (Wagner)
(XPh 1524) 14-12-05 F. 39408

HMB 83 Francesco NAVARINI (bs) (with un-named tenor)
Lucrezia Borgia : Separarsi al alba ... Vieni, la mia vendetta (Donizetti)
(XPh 2397) 1- 2-07 F. 62026 *HRS 1023*
Lucrezia Borgia : Qualunque sia l'evento (Donizettti)
(XPh 2398) 1- 2-07 F. 62027 *HRS 1023*

HMB 84 Julia CULP (c)
Verborgenheit (Wolf)
(xB 2177) -12-06 Od. 64005
Du bist die Ruh' (Schubert)
(xB 2181) -12-06 Od. 64006

HMA 85 Francesco TAMAGNO (t)
Samson et Dalila : Figli miei, v'arrestate (Arrêtez, ô mes frères !) (Saint-Saëns)
(3018 FT (b)) - 2-03 G. Unp. Ist.Issue
Mattia BATTISTINI (b)
Demon : Deh non plorar (Rubinstein)
(446 z) 1902 G. 52670 *IRCC 143*

HMB 86 Ekaterina Mefodievna POPOVA (s)
Mikhail Nikolayevich KARAKASH (b)
Eugene Onegin : Final Duet (1) (R) (Tchaikovsky)
(2886½ c) 30-10-13 G. 024080
Eugene Onegin : Final duet (2) (R) (Tchaikovsky)
(2887 c) 30-10-13 G. 024081

HMA 87 Maria DE MACCHI (s)
Norma : Casta diva (Bellini)
(XPh 478) 19-11-05 F. 39495
Norma : Ah ! bello a me ritorna (Bellini)
(XPh 484) 22-11-05 F. 39496

HMA 88 Francesco VIÑAS (t)
Aïda : Celeste Aïda (Verdi)
(XPh 161) 22- 2-05 F. 39136 *PO 110*
L'Africaine : O paradiso (Ô paradis) (Meyerbeer)
(XPh 170) 20- 2-05 F. 39134 *PO 110*

HMA 89 Elsa BLAND (s) Leo SLEZAK (t)
Die Königin von Saba : Kommst du endlich wieder (Goldmark)
(13226 u) 1908 G. 2-44426
Il Trovatore : Miserere (G) (Verdi)
(10864 u) - 6-07 G. 2-44242

HMB 90 Elena RUSZKOWSKA (s)
Stabat Mater : Inflammatus (Rossini)

		(1813 c)	27- 4-09	G. 053250	
	La Forza del Destino : La vergine degl'angeli (Verdi)				
		(1807 c)	24- 4-09	G. 053237	
HMA	91	Feodor Ivanovich CHALIAPIN (bs)			
	The Prisoner (R) (Rubinstein)				
		(5301 ae)	12- 1-14	G. Unp. Ist.Issue	
	A Word of Farewell (R) (Slonov)				
		(5300 ae)	12- 1-14	G. Unp. Ist.Issue	
HMB	92	Elizavyeta Fiodorovna PETRENKO (c)			
	Demon : Do not swear, but love me (R) (Rubinstein)				
		(2056 c)	11-10-10	G. 024051	
	Samson et Dalila : Amour ! viens aider ma faiblesse (R) (Saint-Saëns)				
		(2041 c)	27- 9-10	G. 023065	
HMA	93	Emma CARELLI (s)			
	Manon : Ancor son io tutt'attonita (Je suis encore) (Massenet)				
		(XPh 1820)	23- 4-06	F. 39650	
		FELIA LITVINNE (s)			
	Lohengrin : Rêve d'Elsa (Einsam in trüben Tagen) (Wagner)				
		(XPh 676)	[1906]	F. 39182	*IRCC T*
HMA	94	Germaine LUBIN (s) Gerard SOUZAY (b)			
	Signes (Leguerney)				
		(0LA 4303-1)	25- 4-44	G. Unp. Ist.Issue	
	Per valli, per boschi (Blangini)				
		(0LA 4302-1)	25- 4-44	G. Unp. Ist.Issue	
HMB	95	Viktoria Viktorovna KAVETSKAYA (s)			
	The Nightingale (R) (Alyabyev)				
		(2445 c)	25- 9-11	G. 023085	
		Feodor Ivanovich CHALIAPIN (bs)			
	Askold's Tomb : In golden days of our forefathers (R) (Verstovsky)				
		(2007 c)	26- 8-10	G. Unp. Ist.Issue	
HMA	96	Antonina Vasilyevna NEZHDANOVA (s)			
	Matushka golobushka (R) (Gurilev)				
		(16400 b)	17- 4-12	G. 2-23651	
	Ruslan and Ludmila : Ah destiny (R) (Glinka)				
		(2710 r)	1906	G. 2-23131	
HMB	97	Dmitri Alexeyevich SMIRNOV (t)			
	Sadko : Song of the Indian Guest (R) (Rimsky-Korakov)				
		(2542½ c)	20-11-11	G. 022240	
		Dinh GILLY (b)			
	Hérodiade : Ce breuvage ... Vision fugitive (Massenet)				
		(Cc 3344-1)	22- 8-23	G. (2-032075)	
HMB	98	Vasili Petrovich DAMAEV (t)			
	Sadko : Ho, faithful friends (R) (Rimsky-Korsakov)				

(2178 c) 1- 2-11 G. 022194
Sadko : As if I had a chest of gold (R) (Rimsky-Korsakov)
(247 af) 19-11-12 G. 022298

HMB 99 Elena Klimentyeva KATULSKAYA (s)
Evgeni Eduardovich WITTING (t)
Sadko : Sea Princess - Sadko Duo (R) (Rimsky-Korsakov)
(2674 c) 17-10-12 G. 024063
Evgeni Eduardovich WITTING (t)
Nyzhegorodzy : Hello, Kremlin (R) (Napravnik)
(2048 c) 30- 9-10 G. 022178

HMB 100 Dame Nellie MELBA (s)
Pur dicesti (Armino) (Lotti)
(4214 f) 19- 5-10 G. Unp. Ist.Issue
Don César de Bazin : A Séville belles señoras (Massenet)
(4184 f) 11- 5-10 G. Unp. Ist.Issue

HMA 101 Matteo DRAGONI (b)
Gianni Schicchi : Intesta la Capellina (Puccini)
(BE 339-1) 28- 3-22 G. 7-52209
Il Tabarro : Scorri, fiume eterno (Puccini)
(BE 342-2) 28- 3-22 G. 7-52211

HMB 102 Alice GUSZALEWICZ (s) Lauritz MELCHIOR (t)
Die Walküre : Siegmund heiss'ich (Wagner)
(CLR 4276-3) 19- 6-28 G. EJ.300
Lauritz MELCHIOR (t)
Die Walküre : Ein Schwert verheiss mir der Vater (Wagner)
(CLR 4725-2) 19- 6-28 G. EJ.300

HMB 103 Hanna GRANFELT (s)
Ruusu Pieni (Little Rose) (Kilpinen)
(BE 1572-2) 18- 5-29 G. X.3134
Äidin Silmät (Mother's eyes) (Hannikainen)
(BE 1573-1) 18- 5-29 G. X.3134

HMB 104 Dmitri Alexeyevich SMIRNOV (t)
Lohengrin : In fernem Land (R) (Wagner)
(2471 c) 9-11-11 G. 022214
Les Pêcheurs de Perles : Je crois entendre encore (R) (Bizet)
(434½ s) -11-09 G. 022143

HMA 105 Lilli LEHMANN (s)
Don Giovanni : Non mi dir, bell'idol mio (Mozart)
(xB 3045) 22- 6-07 Od. Ux 52575 *DST E*
Don Giovanni : Fors' è un giorno il cielo (Mozart)
(xB 3046) 22- 6-07 Od. Ux 52576 *DST E*

HMB 106 Clarence WHITEHALL (bs-b)
Minnie SALTZMANN-STEVENS (c)

Die Walküre : Seek not, o Maid, my spirit to vanquish (Wagner)
(2812 f) 12- 2-09 G. 04041
Peter CORNELIUS (t) Minnie SALTZMAN-STEVENS (s)
Die Walküre : Wer bist du, sag (Wagner)
(2819 f) 12- 2-09 G. 044107

HMB 107 Maria TURIGLIA (s) Matteo DRAGONI (b)
Andrea Chénier : Se ancor di me (Giordano)
(CE 394-1) 20-12-22 G. 2-054122
Matteo DRAGONI (b)
Andrea Chénier : Un dì m'era di gioia (Giordano)
(3307 c) 1-10-18 G. 2-052132

HMB 108 Natalia Stepanova ERMOLENKO-YUZHINA (s)
Madama Butterfly: Un bel dì vedremo (R) (Puccini)
(2509½ c) 28-10-11 G. 023089
Der Fliegende Holländer : Senta's Ballad (R) (Wagner)
(2519 c) 31-10-11 G. 023110

HMA 109 Lotte SCHÖNE (s)
La Bohème : Donde lieta usci (Puccini)
(0D 258) 20- 3-31 G. DA.1238
L'Invito (Bolero) (Rossini)
(0D 260) 20- 3-31 G. DA.1238

HMB 110 Eugenia Adalfovna BRONSKAYA (s)
Life for the Czar : I do not grieve (R) (Glinka)
(2882 c) 29-10-13 G. 023150
Zabava Putyatishna : Zabava's aria (R) (Ivanov)
(283½ af) 18- 1-14 G. 023151

HMB 111 Luisa TETRAZZINI (s)
Somewhere a voice is calling (Tate)
(HO 548½ c) 20- 6-14 G. Unp. 1st. Issue
La Serenata (Leggenda Valacca) (Braga)
(HO 554½ c) 20- 6-14 G. Unp. 1st. Issue

HMB 112 Blanche Lavin DE CASAS (ms) Elena RUSZKOWSKA (s)
Aïda : Fu la sorte dell'armi (Verdi)
(1860 c) 1-11-09 G. 054272
Aïda : Ebben, qual nuovo fremito (Verdi)
(1861 c) 1-11-09 G. 054273

HMB 113 Blanche Lavin DE CASAS (ms) Elena RUSZKOWSKA (s)
Aïda : Ah ! Pietà di prendi (Verdi)
(1862 c) 1-11-09 G. 054276
Blanche Lavin DE CASAS (ms)
Le Prophète : Pietà (Complainte de la mendiante) (Meyerbeer)
(2727 f) 21-11-08 G. 053203

HMB 114 Julius PATZAK (t)

Schwanengesang : Ihr Bild (Schubert D.957)
(CHA 985) 5-12-47 Col. Unp. Ist.Issue
Das Lied im Grunen (Schubert D.917)
(CHA 984) 5-12-47 Col.Unp. Ist.Issue

HMB 115 Lev Mikhailovich SIBIRYAKOV (bs)
Ernani : Infelice ! e tu credevi (R) (Verdi)
(2031 c) 20- 9-10 G. 022172
Lohengrin : Mein Herr und Gott (R) (Wagner)
(2033 c) 20- 9-10 G. 022175

HMA 116 Oskar Isaevich KAMIONSKY (b)
Zazà : Zazà piccola zingara (R) (Leoncavallo)
(18366 b) 26-11-13 G. Unp. Ist.Issue
Mikhail Nikolayevich KARAKASH (b)
Eugene Onegin : Onegin's aria A1 (*Written words)* (R) (Tchaikovsky)
(18028 b) 25-10-13 G. Unp.

HMA 117 Francesco TAMAGNO (t)
Le Prophète : Re del cielo (Roi du ciel) (Meyerbeer)
(3006 b) - 2-03 G. Unp. Ist.Issue
Andrea Chénier : Improvviso (Giordano)
(3007 b) - 2-03 G. Unp. Ist.Issue

HMA 118 Geraldine FARRAR (s)
Roland von Berlin : Fahr wohl ! trautgesell (Leoncavallo)
(2496 L) 1904 G. 43632 *IRCC 132*
Ignacy DYGAS (t)
Cavalleria Rusticana : Siciliana (Mascagni)
(1773 ae) - 9-10 G. X 2-62716

HMA 119 Dmitri Alexeyevich SMIRNOV (t)
Lakmé: Ah ! viens dan la forêt profonde (Delibes)
(17943 b) 14-10-13 G. Unp. Ist.Issue
Snegurochka : Cavatina of Tsar Berendy (R) (Rimsky-Korsakov)
(17935 b) 14-10-13 G. Unp. Ist.Issue

HMA 120 Vladimir Ivanovich KASTORSKY (bs)
The Queen of Spades : Tomsky's aria A1 (R) (Tchaikovsky)
(4992 L) 1907 G. 3-22554
A Life for the Tsar : They guess the truth (R) (Glinka)
(4959 L) 1907 G.3-22565

HMA 121 Graziella PARETO (s)
Estrellita (Ponce)
(BS 2260-1) 6- 2-26 G. DA.772
Mi Niña (Guetary)
(BS 2252-1) 6- 2-26 G. DA.772

HMB 122 Antonina Vasolyevna NEZHDANOVA (s)
Les Huguenots : Nobles Siegneurs, salut (R) (Meyerbeer)

(318 af) 13- 4-14 G. 023154
Parla (R) (Arditi)
(2605 c) 24- 4-12 G. 023106

HMB 123 Gota LJUNGBERG (s)
Tosca : Vissi d'arte (Puccini)
(CLR 5421-2) 28- 5-29 G. D.2019
Gota LJUNGBERG (s) Josef SCHMIDT (t)
Tosca : Nur deinetwegen wollt (Amaro sol per te) (Puccini)
(CLR 5422-2) 28- 5-29 G. D..2019

HMA 124 Maria CANIGLIA (s)
Stornello (Poesia popolare toscana)
(0BA 1401-1) 25- 5-36 G. DA.1497
Mi madre se midate giovannino (Giuranna)
(0BA 1428-1) 2- 6-36 G. DA.1497

HMB 125 Gerhard HUSCH (b)
Schwanengesang : Die Taubenpost (Schubert)
(2RA 2185) 27- 8-37 G. Unp. Ist.Issue
Schwanengesang : Abschied (Schubert)
(2RA 2187) 27- 8-37 G. Unp. Ist.Issue

HMA 126 Avelina CARRERA (s)
Cavalleria Rusticana : Voi lo sapete (Mascagni)
(XPh 3063) 11- 3-08 F. 92169
Siberia : Nel suo amore rianimato (Giordano)
(XPh 3115) 3- 4-08 F. 92168

HMA 127 Feodor Ivanovich CHALIAPIN (bs)
On the Hills of Georgia (R) (Rimsky-Korsakov op.3 No.4)
(5303 ae) 12- 1 14 G. Unp. Ist.Issue
A Swan (R) (Grieg op.25 No.2)
(5302 ae) 12- 1-14 G. Unp. Ist.Issue

HMB 128 Alexandr Dormidontovich ALEXANDROVITCH (t)
Elena Klimentyeva KATULSKAYA (s)
Faust : Il se fait tard (R) (Gounod)
(2783½ c) 5- 4-13 G. 023076
Faust : Éternelle (R) (Gounod)
(2784 c) 5- 4-13 G. 024077

HMB 129 Walter WIDDOP (t)
Maritana : Yes, let me like a soldier fall (Wallace)
(Cc 18617-4) 23- 1-30 G. D.1887
Faust : All hail ! Thou dwelling (Salut ! demeure chaste et pure)(Gounod)
(Cc 17998-3) 11- 3-30 G. D.1887

HMA 130 Mary LOSSEFF Richard TAUBER (t)
Der Singende Traum : Sagen dir nicht meine Augen (Tauber)
(Ve 2136-2) 1934 Od. O-4541

		Der Singende Traum : Sing mir ein Liebeslied (Tauber)		
		(Ve 2139-2)	1934	Od. O-4541
HMA	131	Florence EASTON (s)		
		Songs my mother taught me (Dvorak)		
		(0B 5558-1)	18- 1-34	G. Unp. Ist.Issue
		Hat dich die Liebe berührt (Marx)		
		(0B 5561-1)	18- 1-34	G. Unp. 1st. Issue *IRCC 174*
HMA	132	Giuseppe DI STEFANO (t)		
		Mamma (Bixio)		
		(0ZA 1239)	1944	G. JK.34
		Se vuoi goder la vita (Bixio)		
		(0ZA 1240)	1944	G. JK.34
HMA	133	Ria GINSTER (s)		
		Die Zauberflöte : Ach, ich fühls (Mozart)		
		(0B 4194)	13- 1-33	G. DA.1326
		Le Nozze di Figaro : Non so più cosa son (Mozart)		
		(0B 6401)	13- 1-33	G. DA.1326
HMB	134	Gerhard HUSCH (b)		
		Schwanengesang : Am Meer (Schubert)		
		(2RA 2188-1)	27- 8-37	G. Unp. Ist.Issue
		Schwanengesang : Die Doppelgänger (Schubert)		
		(2RA 2189-1)	27- 8-37	G. Unp. Ist.Issue
HMB	135	Evgeni Eduardovich WITTING (t)		
		La Gioconda : Cielo e mar ! (R) (Ponchielli)		
		(2541 c)	-11-11	G. 022239
		Evgeni Eduardovich WITTING (t) Alexandr Mikhailovich BRAGIN (b) Lev Mikhailovich SIBIRYAKOV (bs)		
		Faust : Que voulez-vous Messieurs ? (R) (Gounod)		
		(2036 c)	- 9-10	G. 024040
HMB	136	Florence AUSTRAL (s)		
		Love's old sweet song (Molloy)		
		(Cc 18987)	27- 3-30	G. Unp Ist.Issue.
		Maritana : Scenes that are brightest (Wallace)		
		(Bb 18988)	27- 3-30	G. Unp. Ist.Issue
HMA	137	Elisabeth SCHUMANN (s)		
		Wie glanzt der Helle Mond (Wolf)		
		(0EA 10779-5)	2-10-48	G. Unp. Ist.Issue
		Nimmersatte (Wolf)		
		(0EA 10781-1)	27-11-45	G. Unp. Ist.Issue
HMB	138	Hina SPANI (s)		
		Otello : Salce (Willow song) (Verdi)		

(CF 1626-2) 3- 4-38 G. Unp. Ist.Issue

HM (A) 138 Hina SPANI (s)

Guillaume Tell : Sombre forêt (Rossini)

(0F 168-3) 7- 7-31 G. Unp. Ist.Issue

HMA 139 Helge ROSWAENGE (t)

Balkanliebe : Heimsallied (Kattrigg)

(0RA 2462-1) 19-11-37 G. EG.6165

Balkanliebe : Barcarolle (Kattrigg)

(0RA 2463-1) 19-11-37 G. EG.6165

HMB 140 Nikolai Artemyevich SHEVELEV (b)

Quo Vadis : O triomphe (R) (Nougués)

(2525 c) 31-10-11 G. 022250

Henry V111: Qui donc commande (R) (Saint-Saëns)

(2526 c) 31-10-11 G. 022251

HMB 141 Eugenia Adalfovna BRONSKAYA (s)

Mignon : Polonaise (Je suis Titania) (R) (Thomas)

(2778 c) 19-10-12 G. Unp. Ist.Issue

Nadezhda Timofeyevna VAN BRANDT (s)

La Zingara : Fra l'erbe cosparse (R) (Donizetti)

(6718 p) 1907 G. 023023

HMB 142 Evgeniya Ivanovna ZBRUYEVA (c)

Rogneda : Izjaslav's entreaty (R) (Serov)

(2923 c) -11-13 G. 023145

A Life for the Czar : I do not grieve (R) (Glinka)

(2660 c) -10-12 G. 023119

HMB 143 Walter WIDDOP (t)

The Death of Nelson (Braham)

(Cc 18619-4) 11- 3-30 G. D.1833

Tom Bowling (Dibdin)

(Cc 18618-3) 11- 3-30 G. D.1833

HMB 144 Lilli LEHMANN (s) Hedwig HELBIG (s)

Così fan Tutte : Ich erwähle mir den Muntern (Prenderò quel Brunettino) (Mozart)

(xB 3061) 25- 6-07 Od. 50397 *DST F*

Lilli LEHMANN (s)

La Traviata : Alfredo, Alfredo, in questo core (Verdi)

(xB 3047) 22- 6-07 Od. 50374 *DST F*

HMB 145 Dmitri Alexeyevich SMIRNOV (t)

Les Huguenots : Plus blanche que la blanche hermine (Meyerbeer)

(2681 c) 19-10-12 G. Unp. Ist.Issue

Tranquility (R) (Kazhevarov)

(2546 c) 20-11-11 G. 022241

HMA 146 Luigi SIMONETTA-RANGONI (t)

Nebbie (Respighi)

(20454 b) 2- 5-19 G. 7-52129

Quando ti vidi (Wolf-Ferrari)

Io dei salute (Wolf-Ferrari)

(20433 b) 29- 4-19 G. 7-52130

HMB 147 Dame Nellie MELBA (s)

Tosca : Vissi d'arte (Puccini)

(4186 f) 11- 5-10 G. Unp. Ist.Issue

The sounds of earth grow faint (Ronald)

(4194 f) 11- 5-10 G. Unp. Ist.Issue

HMB 148 Clara BUTT (c)

Peace and rest (Batten)

(4554 f) 28-10-10 G. Unp. Ist.Issue

Land of Hope and Glory (Elgar)

(4974 f) 24- 4-11 G. Unp. Ist.Issue

HMB 149 Otto TAMINI (t)

Die Walküre : Winterstürme (Wagner)

(2786 f) 21- 1-09 G. 042190

Ernest VAN DYCK (t)

Du bist wie eine Blume (Schumann)

(XPh 539) 1905 F. 39101

HMB 150 Pavel Ilyitch TIKHONOV (bs)

Tannhäuser : Landgrave's Monologue (R) (Wagner)

(2789 c) 17- 4-13 G. 022330

A Life for the Tsar : They guess the truth (R) (Glinka)

(2788c) 17-4-13 G. 022321

HMA 151 Graziella PARETO (s)

a) *L'heure riera* (Trad.) b) *Bon cacador* (Trad.)

(Bs 2250-2) 5- 2-26 G. DA.781

a) *La Pastoretta* (Trad.) b) *Canco de nadal* (Trad.)

(Bs 2251-1) 5- 2-26 G. DA.781

HMB 152 Paul FRANZ (t)

Parsifal : Hagards mes yeux (6 bars before *Es starrt der Blick*)(Wagner)

(02883 v) 10- 1-14 G. 032303

Les Huguenots : Plus blanche que la blanche hermine (Meyerbeer)

(02616 v) 7-12-12 G. 032268

HMB 153 Marta FUCHS (s)

Schwanengesang : In der ferme (Schubert)

(0RA 2202) 29- 8-37 G. Unp. 1st. Issue

Aufenhalt (Schubert)

(0RA 2201) 29- 8-37 G. Unp. 1st. Issue

HMB 154 Selma KURZ (s)

Il Re Pastore : L'amerò, sarò, constante (Mozart)

(Cc 4736-4) 25- 6-24 G. 2-043046

Die Zauberflöte : O zittre nicht ... Zum leiden (Mozart)
(Cc 4768-1) 24- 6-24 G. Unp. 1st. Issue
HMB 155 Antonina NESHDANOVA (s)
Ruslan and Ludmilla : Ludmilla's aria : Ah, destiny (R) (Glinka)
(2710 r) 1907 G. 2-23131
A Life for the Tsar : I do not grieve (R) (Glinka)
(2718 r) 1907 G. 2-23140
HMB 156 Alexandr ALEXANDROVICH (t)
Orfeo : Chiamo il mio ben così (R) (Gluck)
(2786 c) 5- 4-13 G. 022311
Orfeo : Che farò senza Euridice (R) (Gluck)
(2770 c) 2- 4-13 G. 022310
Note: Numbers HM 157 to 170 are projected issues as we go to press.
HMA 157 Ignacy DYGAS (t)
I Pagliacci : Vesti la giubba (Pol.) (Leoncavallo)
(1770 ae) * - 9-10 G. 222073
* Another take with the same number issued on X-2-62567
Elena Klimentyeva KATULSKAYA (s)
La Bohème : Quando m'en vo' (R) (Puccini)
(5952 ae) 10- 4-14 G. Unp. 1st. Issue
HMB 158 Walter WIDDOP (t) Gota LJUNGBERG (s)
Tannhäuser : Venus Duet (Pt.1) (Wagner)
(Cc 20643 -1) 28-10-30 G. (32-1873) Ist.Issue
Walter WIDDOP (t) Florence AUSTRAL (s) Chorus
Götterdämmerung : Helle Wehr (Wagner)
(Cc 13728 -3A) 17-10-28 G. D.1579 DB.4659
HMB 159 Herbert JANSSEN (b)
Ganymed (Schubert)
(2EA 6153) 22- 3-38 G. Unp. 1st. Issue
Kriegers Ahnung (Schubert)
(2RA 2199) 29- 8-37 G. Unp. 1st. Issue
HMB 160 Bernardo DE MURO (t) Maria ROGGERO
Ruy Blas : O dolce voluttà (Marchetti)
(753 m) 4- 4-14 G. 054479
Bernardo DE MURO (t)
Andrea Chénier : Un dì all'azzuro spazio (Giordano)
(3186 c) 23- 5-17 G. 2-052174
HMB 161 Elena GERHARDT (s)
Paride ed Elena : O del mio dolce ardor (It) (Gluck)
(1311 s) 13- 1-14 G. 043261
Elena GERHARDT (s) NIKISCH (pno)
An die Musik (Schubert)
(ac 5112 f) 30- 6-11 G. 043202

HMB 162 Vera Nikolayevna PETROVA - SVANTSEVA (ms)
Vasili Petrovich DAMAEV (t)
Samson et Dalila : Mon coeur s'ouvre (Saint-Saëns)
(1923 c) 25- 1-10 G. 024033
Vasili Petrovich DAMAEV (t)
Oprichnik : Proshanie Morozov (Tchaikovsky)
(2926 c) 15-12-13 G. Unp. 1st. Issue

HMB 163 Ivar ANDRESEN (bs)
Götterdämmerung: Ihr Gibichsmannen, machet euch auf ! (Wagner)
(CDR 4708-2) 21-6-27 G. D. 1578
Götterdämmerung: Schlugen wir Tierre (Wagner)
(CDR 4709-1) 21-6-27 G. D. 1579
HMA 164 Francesco TAMAGNO (t)
Hérodiade : Quand nos jours (Massenet)
(3022 FT (b)) - 2-03 G. Unp. 1st. Issue
Emanuele CIGADA (b) Clara JOANNA (s)
Antonio PAOLI (t)
Il Trovatore : Di geloso amor sprezzato (Verdi)
(10519 b) 1907 G. 54340
HMB 165 Celestina BONINSEGNA (t) Luigi BOLIS (t)
Loreley: Lascia per or che libera (Catalani)
(3197 c) 2- 6-17 G. 2-053136
Il Guarany : Pery ! Che brami ? ... Sento una forza indomita (Gomez)
(3198 c) 2- 6-17 G. 2-054087
HMB 166 Edward LLOYD (t)
The Minstrel Boy (Moore)
(1974 f) 1907 G. 02101
a) *Songs my mother taught me* (Dvorak)
b) *Tune thy strings, o gypsy* (Dvorak)
(2049 f) 1907 G. 02118
HMB 167 Dinh GILLY (b)
Hérodiade : Vision fugitive (Massenet)
(Cc 3344-2) 22- 8-23 2-032075
N.B. HMB 97 has Cc 3344-**1**
Ninon VALLIN (s) Paul PAYAN (bs)
Louise : Louise - Father duet (*Berceuse* Pt. 2) (Charpentier)
(02947 v) 15- 4-14 G. Unp. 1st. Issue
HMA 168 Conchita SUPERVIA (ms)
Should he upbraid (Bishop)
(WLO 3003) c. 3-32 Od. 184.315
Florence EASTON (s)
My mother bids me bind my hair (Haydn)

		(0B 5557-1)	18- 1-34	G. Unp. V. 1705
HMB	169	Vladimir ROSING (t)		
		Carmen : La fleur (R) (Bizet)		
		(2712 c)	3-12-12	G. Unp. 1st. Issue
		Eugene Onegin : Lensky's Aria A.2 (R) (Tchaikovsky)		
		(2713 c)	3-12-12	G. Unp. 1st. Issue
HMB	170	Emmy DESTINN (s) Louise Kirkby LUNN (ms)		
		La Gioconda : L'amo come il fulgor del creato (Ponchielli)		
		(5144 f)	6- 7-11	G.2-054020X
		Aïda : Ebben, qual nuovo fremito (Verdi)		
		(5145 f)	6- 7-11	G. 2 054023

CROSS INDEX

BALDISSERI Nerina	VB 46
BARBIERI Elvira	VB 69 // HM 5
BARRIENTOS Maria	IRCC D // PO 76
BATTISTINI Mattia	IRCC 77 - 143 - 202 // HRS 1007 // AGSA 24 - 30 - 31 // AGSB 4 - 52 (AGSB) 93 - 94 // ABHB 1 - 2 - 4 // DGG PM 85061 // 15_ 1010 // VA 5 - 15 - 65 // VB 14 - 18 - 23 - 49 - 63 - 69 // HM 5 - 47 - 85
BAUERMEISTER Mathilde	IRCC 177
BELLINCIONI Gemma	VB 11
BERGAMINI Lamberto	HM 38
BISPHAM David	IRCC 59 - 152
BLAND Elsa	HM 89
BLASS Robert	IRCC 115
BLAUVELT Lillian	IRCC 8 // AGSA 4
BOCCOLINI Ebe	HM 47
BOEMI A.	AGSB 20
BOLIS Luigi	IRCC 84 // VB 4 - 27 // HM 165
BONCI Alessandro	IRCC C // HRS 1022 // PXO 87
BONINSEGNA Celestina	IRCC 15 - 63 - 84 - 142 // 15_1006 // VA 4 - 10 / VB 4 - 11 - 27 - 28 // HM 44 165
BORGATTI Giuseppe	HM 82
BORI Lucrezia	IRCC 70 // HRS 1039 // AGSB 58 // 15_1009 // VA 17 // HM 44
BORONAT Olympia	IRCC 50 - 56 - 180 // 15_1023 // VA 11 - 19 // VB 10 / HM 20 - 29 - 65
BRAGIN Alexandr	HM 135
BREVAL Lucienne	IRCC 183
BRIDEWELL Carrie	IRCC 163 - 177
BRONSKAYA Eugenia	HM 68 - 110 - 141
BROWNLEE John	VB 64
BURZIO Eugenia	HRS 1029 // PO 136
BUTT Clara	AGSB 75 // HM 31 - 148
CAHIER Mme.Charles	IRCC 162 // HM 69
CALVÉ Emma	IRCC 5 - 163 // AGSB 6 - 46
CAMPANARI Giuseppe	IRCC 86 - 163
CANIGLIA Maria	HM 124
CARELLI Emma	HM 93
CARON Rose	HRS 1019
CARRERA Avelina	HM 126
CARUSO Enrico	IRCC 36 - 61 // AGSA 2 - 27 // AGSB 18 - 50 // D.G.G P 80007 D.G.G. PM 85012 // 15_1004 - 15_1019 - 15_1025 - 15_1036 to 15_1040 16_5000 to 16_5003 // VA 7 - 9 - 12 - 29 to 45 - 53 - 58 //

DEMUTH Leopold	IRCC L
DESTINN Emmy	IRCC H - J - 16 - 36 - 51 - 65 - 82 - 147 - 184 // AGSB 12 - 48 // PXO 84 // 15_1014 // VB 24 - 25 // HM 55 - 170
DEVRIES David	AGSA 17
DIDUR Adamo	PO 69
DIPPEL Andreas (t)	IRCC 110 - 163
DI STEFANO Giuseppe	HM 132
DOMGRAF-FASSBAENDER Willi	AGSB 10
DONALDA Pauline	IRCC 46 // AGSA 4 // VB 10
DRAGONI Matteo	HM 40 - 101 - 107
DUCHENE Maria	AGSA 17 // AGSB 73 // 16_5000 // VA 28
DUMENSIL Suzanne	AGSA 17 // AGSB 73
DUPOY Louis	V. 15_1026
DYGAS Ignacy	HM 118 - 157
EAMES Emma	IRCC 20 - 32 - 43 - 44 - 76 - 90 - 113 - 125 - 179 - 194 - 216 // HRS 1016 // AGSB 5 - 15 - 22 - 60
EASTON Florence	IRCC 174 // HM 131 - 168
EDVINA Marie	VA 48
ELIZZA Elise	VA 57
ERMOLENKO-YUZHINA Natalia	HM 66 - 81 - 108
ESCALAIS Léon	HRS 2008
FARNETI Maria	HM 61 - 67
FARRAR Geraldine	IRCC 1 - 14 - 29 - 30 - 40 - 41 - 45 - 55 - 58 - 61 - 67 - 68 - 79 - 114 - 132 - 156 - 195 - 215 // AGSA 5 // AGSB 25 - 50 - 51 - 55 // 16_5001- 16_5003 // VA 14 // HM 118
FLAGSTAD Kirsten	AGSA 34 - 35
FLETA Miguel	HRS 1039 // AGSB 58 // VB 50
FORNIA Rita	AGSB 61
FORST Grete	VA 57
FRANZ Paul	HM 152
FREMSTAD Olive	IRCC 12 - 74 // AF 2 - 3
FUCHS Marta	HM 153
FUGÈRE Lucien	HM 14
GADSKI Johanna	IRCC 26 - 42 - 121 - 128 - 140 - 146 - 164 - 168 - 177 - 186 - 201 // HRS 1008 - 1047 // AGSA 36 // AGSB 12 - 23 - 36 // VB 52
GALLI-CURCI Amelita	HRS 1031 // AGSB 80 // VA 8 // VB 5 - 65 - 66
GALVANY Maria	IRCC F - K - 64 - 92 - 104 // HRS 1010 // VA 4 - 46 // VB 4 - 26 - 68

	ABHA 1 // 15_1003- 15_1026 // 16_5000 - 16_5002 - 16_5003 // VA 23 - 47 - 71 // VB 30 - 71
JUCH Emma	1RCC 23
KAMIONSKY Oskar	HM 116
KARAKASH Mikhail	HM 50 - 79 - 86 - 116
KASTORSKY Vladimir	HM 26 - 80 - 120
KATULSKAYA Elena	HM 27 - 99 - 128 - 157
KAVETSKAYA Viktoria	HM 33 - 56 - 95
KITTEL Hermine	VA 57
KLEMENTIEV Lev	HM 68
KNUPFER Paul	IRCC 91
KOVALENKO Maria	AGSB 8
KRAUS Ernst	VB 25
KRUSCENISCI Salomea	IRCC W // HRS 1017 // PO 132
KURT Melanie	IRCC 91 - 124 // HM 35 - 39
KURZ Selma	IRCC L - 165 // AGSA 18 // AGSB 47 // ABHB 5 // VA 2 // VB 2 - 35 - 48 // HM 6 - 22 - 42 - 154
LABINSKY Andrei	HM 79
LAURI VOLPI Giacomo	AGSA 28 // AGSB 57
LEHMANN Lilli	See DST / Gramophone series + IRCC M - P - Q - R - 37 // PO 63 // HM 59 - 60 - 105 - 144
LEIDER Frida	AGSB 26
LEJEUNE Gabrielle	AGSA 17 // AGSB 73
LELIWA Tadeusz	PO 125
LEROUX F. (t)	AGSA 17 // AGSB 73
LIPKOVSKAYA Lydia	HM 41
LITVINNE Felia	IRCC S - T // HMB 10 - 93
LJUNGBERG Gota	HM 123 - 158
LLOYD Edward	HM 166
LOSSEFF Mary	HM 130
LUBIN Germaine	HM 71 - 94
LUNN Louise Kirkby	IRCC 36 - 147 // AGSB 21 // HM 170
LUPPI Oreste	HRS 2008 // PO 119 - 139
MAGINI-COLETTI Antonio	HRS 1024 - 2008 // PO 119 - 133
MANTELLI Eugenia	IRCC 77- 5008
MANURITTA Giovanni	HM 30
MARCHESI Blanche	IRCC 89 - 97 - 119
MARCONI Francesco	VB 4 - 27
MARDONES José	AGSB 27
MARILLY Marguerite	IRCC 177
MARION Gloria	AGSB 20
MARTIN Riccardo	IRCC 117 // HRS 1002 - 2006 // 15_1029